Phil Lempert's

Getting the Most

Supermarket

for Your Money

Shopping and

in Every Aisle

Value Guide

Phil Lempert

The Supermarket Guru™

CB

CONTEMPORARY BOOKS

A TRIBUNE NEW MEDIA/EDUCATION COMPANY

Library of Congress Cataloging-in-Publication Data

Lempert, Phil.
   Phil Lempert's supermarket shopping and value guide:
   getting the most for your money in every aisle / Phil
   Lempert.
         p.   cm.
   Includes bibliographical references.
   ISBN 0-8092-3203-0
   1. Marketing (Home economics)—United States.
I. Title.
TX356.L46   1996
640'.73—dc20   95-51970
                                                 CIP

Cover design by Kim Bartko
Interior design and production by Susan H. Hartman

Published by Contemporary Books, Inc.
Two Prudential Plaza, Chicago, Illinois 60601-6790
Manufactured in the United States of America
International Standard Book Number: 0-8092-3203-0
10   9   8   7   6   5   4   3   2

This book is dedicated to

my father, Sol,
for teaching me to aim my dreams high

my mother, Lillian,
for believing in my dreams and nurturing them

and

my wife, Laura,
for helping me realize my dreams.

CONTENTS

Chapter 2

Chapter 3

Chapter 6

Chapter 7

Chapter 8

ACKNOWLEDGMENTS

Supermarkets carefully select many thousands of products, then present them together to create a fabulous experience for the shopper. So has it been in the preparation of this book. I serve as your guide to the information and shopping hints shared by thousands of consumers, supermarket retailers, and manufacturers who care about creating the ultimate supermarket shopping experience. I thank them all for their insights and passion.

I would especially like to thank the many people at Tribune Company who strongly believe in the need to convey accurate, quality information to our hundreds of millions of readers, viewers, and listeners throughout the United States and across all media. Their foresight and continued support in the formation of The Supermarket Alliance will help the food industry and our supermarkets grow even further. Jim Dowdle, David Hiller, Cathy Jaros, and Lisa Wiersma have helped polish the concept and enabled me to maximize my vision of consumer trends and the supermarket. Owen Youngman, Janet Franz, Carol Haddix, Renee Enna, Mike Silver, Walter Mahoney, T. Allan Smith, Mike Dreadon, Sheri Enix, Jim Disch, Steve Dolinsky, and Nelson Howard have all consistently offered their ideas, insights, and support, and I thank you.

A special acknowledgment and thanks must be given to our daily operational team at Tribune Company, which is led by the inspiring Richard Stone and the untiring, supportive, and always dedicated Karen Volkman-Androphy. Along with Nancy Roeder, Pat Yancovitz, and especially Vivien Stern (who many years ago first believed in me and my insights), we have created a unique and valuable resource in bringing together the media and food worlds.

I must thank my colleagues at the *Today* show for allowing me to bring the supermarket and new food products into the homes of tens of millions of viewers every month. No one could ever ask for a better on-camera partner than Bryant Gumbel, whose love and understanding of food, together with his desire for quality, is second to none. My special thanks to Katie Couric, Jeff Zucker, Beth O'Connell, Michael Bass, and in particular, my producer Jason Raff. They are a "class act" team that I am proud to know and work with.

Tom Gillespie and Joe Burke at the Coca-Cola Company deserve acknowledgment for allowing me to bring my insights to supermarket retailers throughout the country. Their commitment to the supermarket industry serves as a model for all. I have benefited from their knowledge, friendship, and humor.

Much of what I share in this book I have learned from working with and hearing the advice of the giants of the supermarket world. In many cases, they have allowed me to test new ideas in their stores, bond with their customers, and frankly and openly discuss their needs and desires. I would like to offer my thanks to them all, particularly Morty and Larri Wolfson and Augie Eberhardt of the Lincoln Park ShopRite, who over the years have proved to be my friends and are brilliant marketing partners. Thanks also to Dean Janeway and Mary Ellen Gowin of Wakefern; Larry Del Santo of Vons; and Joe Pichler, Dick Owens, Pat Kenny, Don Dufek, Dave Dillon, Dick Bere, Bill Parker, Bob Zinke, Mark Thompson, Jim Thorn, Larry LaCroix, and Ted Engle of Kroger for their advice and support of my advertising, marketing, and customer service programs. Thanks to Joe Wood of Roundy's, Greg Gregerson of Gregerson's, Michael Rourke of A&P, Bill Louttit of Grand Union, Diane Maffia of Jewel, and John Templeton of Safeway for sharing their experiences.

Thanks to Ken Dychtwald for sharing his insights into lifestage marketing and the fifty-plus consumer. A very special thanks goes to Information Resources Inc. and to Bob Bergenzer for their continuous assistance.

Bob Mariano of Dominick's has led his team well and has created a fabulous shopping experience for Chicago consumers every day of the week. I thank him for his commitment to consumers and quality operation, as well as for allowing me to use the Dominick's stores as the background for the cover of this book and as one of the most beautiful environments TV segments could have. Thanks also to the people who consistently have helped me and our entire staff: Herb Young, Bob McEvoy, Cory Hedman, Addie Voigt, Dan Andrews, and Van Arp, all of Dominick's.

The supermarket industry is fortunate to have as its two major resources the Food Marketing Institute (FMI) and the Grocery Manufacturers of America (GMA). These two trade associations continually strive to serve all aspects of the food industry and do so admirably. Special thanks go to Manly Mopus and Hilarie Hoting of GMA and to Michael Sansolo and Edie Clark of FMI.

Thanks go to Tony D'Amelio and all the wonderful people at the Washington Speakers Bureau for helping me spread the word to the corporate world that the consumer is, and will always be, number one.

To my editor at Contemporary Books, Kara Leverte, my most grateful thanks for her desire to publish this book, her patience and direction with me as a first-time author, and her talents in clarifying and organizing my thoughts. Thank you as well to my art director, Kim Bartko; Gigi Grajdura, our project editor; and to Christine Albritton, publisher, for being an early champion and supporting the publication of this book. Thanks also to my in-field and research team of Laura Gray, Chris McCabe, Felicia Law, Beth Wengrow, and Christy Kim.

The most deserved acknowledgment must be shared with my immediate and extended families for their patience, unwavering belief, and devotion to my dreams. I especially acknowledge my stepson Jeremy, mother-in-law Debbie Bowman, and Barbara, Michael, and Carrie Lubin. Special thanks to a lifelong friend and colleague who is always there with smarts, a smile, and a helpful hand—Kathy Nisivoccia.

Through the support of these people and the tens of thousands of consumers who are willing to share their ideas, I am able to achieve my goal of making the supermarket a better place for us all.

Introduction

I grew up in the food business. My grandfather was a dairy farmer, and my father a food broker, manufacturer, and distributor. Friday nights I shopped with my parents at the Food Fair in Nutley, New Jersey, which for the times (the 1950s) was a big store (about one-third the size of the average supermarket today). It even had a deli!

Our shopping trip, at times to my mom's dismay, was always part business. Each visit to the store included my father's check-in and hellos to each department manager, a review of the new products that had come in that week, and at least one observation of a consumer trying to decide what to buy. Together we would stand back and, by carefully watching that shopper's actions, try to guess which product he or she would select.

With that twenty-one-year internship under my belt, my career began after college. I started out working as a salesman for my dad's food brokerage company, selling foods to the supermarkets in the New York area. That front-line experience taught me well and positioned me to note that food companies and supermarkets were beginning to appreciate the importance of understanding the consumer. Recognizing and then seizing the opportunity, I established an award-winning advertising, marketing, and public relations firm that specialized in (what else?) food products and supermarkets.

Ten years ago I decided that the food industry was ready for and needed much more in-depth understanding of consumers and the trends that affect the marketplace. To share with the industry what I saw and heard from consumers, I began to publish a biweekly newsletter—*The Lempert Report*—containing marketing analysis, issues, and trends.

Today my efforts continue to focus on understanding and identifying consumer and lifestyle trends—as a "food trend consumerologist," if you will. I share these weekly with the readers of my syndicated *Chicago Tribune* newspaper column and through my regular appearances on the *Today* show. To supermarket owners and operators and packaged-goods manufacturers, I report consumer concerns and share observations on the speaker's platform of the major industry conventions, in boardrooms across America, and, of course, through direct contact. What fascinates me is that both supermarket constituencies (consumers and industry) share a strong desire to know much more about the other. That's the good news: otherwise, who knows what tomorrow's supermarket might be—if it existed at all. The bad news is that, according to my rules, the depth of understanding doesn't happen often enough.

Each year I receive thousands of letters and phone calls from shoppers. Armed with those concerns and questions, I visit hundreds of supermarkets throughout the country and talk to thousands more consumers with just one thought in mind: how we can make the supermarket a better place.

I teach supermarket operators that the best way they can find out what we consumers want is to simply ask us. I am not suggesting even one more focus group—but rather talking to one person at a time. Right in the store. Face to face. To succeed, this process must be two-way, and we shoppers are responsible for providing honest and forthright feedback. We also must be proactive. If the supermarkets and manufacturers are not smart enough to ask us what's wrong, we need to tell them!

The supermarket of the future will be more exciting than we can imagine. The combination of technology and our expanding need for human contact and interaction will present us with a new concept of food shopping. I urge each of you to help create this environment by directly communicating with food manufacturers and retailers.

CHAPTER 1

WHAT TO EXPECT (AND NOT TO) FROM YOUR SUPERMARKET

Today's supermarket shopper is smarter and more value conscious than ever before. The free-spending style of the eighties has been replaced with a new style of shopping. Kmart, Wal-Mart, and the local warehouse outlet are suddenly hip places to buy groceries. Bargain hunting, bulk purchasing, and coupon clipping are becoming the national pastime—especially for the seventy-six million baby boomers.

As we witness this "retail revolution," roughly 250 million Americans are reestablishing their shopping habits and experimenting with new products. There is a need and desire—even demand—for high-quality, accurate shopping information. The products we buy must be at the best price possible.

My objective is to share with you my twenty-five years of hands-on experience in the supermarket world. I hope this guide will satisfy the needs of all shoppers in an entertaining, informative, and insightful way. After you read each chapter, I want you to be able to say, "I didn't know that!" and to enjoy your shopping experience a bit more than before.

Based on my thousands of interviews with supermarket shoppers just like you, I can report that there are common needs. Supermarket shoppers, more than consumers of other stores, are constantly in search of a better store, better price, or better value (on average, we visit two different supermarkets a week). Is the supermarket really satisfying our needs so poorly? I don't think so. I do think that—with tens of thousands of products on the shelves, and thousands of new ones trying to get on each year—it's a land of confusion.

The answer is not to keep switching supermarkets (at least not until you've tried all the solutions listed in this book), but rather to understand how your supermarket operates, how to prepare for your weekly shopping trips, and how to choose products. This book is filled with how-tos—everything from creating the ultimate tool (your shopping list) to understanding the new food labels, guaranteeing satisfaction, and, most importantly, saving money on every trip you make to the store.

I want to help you to get the most from your supermarket in terms of value (quality, price, and service) and, most importantly, to enjoy supermarket shopping. You can get satisfaction and have fun on every visit. You just have to know how!

The supermarket in the year 2000 (and beyond) will become even a better place, offering us good nutrition, good information, and a great shopping experience. More and more supermarkets are combining the technological advances of faster (and more accurate) checkouts, preferred-shopper programs, and on-line shopping with freshly prepared meals, in-store coffee bars, and a higher-than-ever degree of personalized service.

DO WE REALLY HATE SUPERMARKETS?

Survey after survey shows that most of us just don't like supermarket shopping. In fact, a recent *Adweek* survey reported that 53 percent of consumers disliked supermarket shopping and 14 percent actually hated it! I can think of no other retail environment that has this many people walking into their stores who don't want to be there.

Why should we have these feelings toward one of the places we visit most often? On average, according to the

Food Marketing Institute (the supermarket industry's trade association), we're at the supermarket 1.7 times per week.

Week after week most of us go into a supermarket that has over 35,000 products. Each week new ones are added, and old ones eliminated. Last year over 20,800 new products were introduced and tried to get on these already overcrowded shelves. Each week a different product is featured at the end of every aisle in larger-than-life displays. Each week hundreds of different products are on sale. In our newspapers and our mailboxes we receive hundreds of coupons every week. Is it possible that we are just a little overwhelmed and intimidated?

Most of us have become friendly with (or at least recognize) a cashier or two, and perhaps we've gotten to know someone in the meat department or deli. Think about how good it makes you feel when they say hello. Or when they alert you to one of your favorite products that just went on sale.

There are benefits of getting to know the people in the store. Besides having a better, more friendly shopping experience, you will also save money. The staff of the store can direct you to new products, store circular coupons, in-store coupons, and rebate offers. They can be your guide to what I tell the supermarket industry is their most important offering: Every Day Value Positioning (EDVP).

We've all seen the in-store banners and ad headlines that proclaim Every Day Low Prices. We've seen the television commercials that show the prices on items falling down, down, down. But with that, at times, we've also seen the level of service and expertise fall as well. We supermarket shoppers want a lot more than just the lowest price. We want a clean store that offers us an assortment of products we want to buy. And what is more important, we also want a pleasant place to shop with smiling people who can answer our questions and solve our problems. None of the consumers I've interviewed have ever told me that they go out of their way to choose a supermarket that is dirty and overpriced and has nasty cashiers who aren't helpful.

Morty and Larri Wolfson own and operate a state-of-the-art ShopRite in Lincoln Park, New Jersey. While their store occupies over sixty thousand square feet, their shoppers feel as if they're inside a neighborhood store. In fact, the store's theme is "just like family"—and they practice it. More often than not, you'll see the family's patriarch, Morty, stationed right alongside the courtesy counter at the entrance, saying hello to his thousands of friends as they come to do their food shopping. Not surprisingly, this store is one of the busiest and most enjoyable supermarkets for miles around.

It would be great if all supermarkets followed the examples set by the Wolfsons and the other successful stores we will visit in the pages of this book. In my thousands of supermarket visits throughout the United States as well as in Italy, Germany, Finland, Holland, Portugal, and China, I've seen it done! Let's move quickly away from today's "hot" concept of piling it high and selling it cheap to "Every Day Value Positioning." True value is the balance of quality, price, selection, and service—the absol' least that we should expect for our money.

How to Get to Know Your Supermarket

How do we get "value" from our supermarkets? It's easier than you may realize. Being familiar with the store is critical. To start on your value expedition, each week for the next six weeks, plan on spending ten extra minutes in the supermarket getting to know a few more people. I promise it will be worth it!

In week 1, introduce yourself to the store's manager or customer service manager and arrange a ten-minute meeting. Taking the time to get to know this person will be well worthwhile. Be organized and focused, using the Store Manager Questionnaire on the next page as a foundation for your meeting. After all, you do have a mission—to become the most important shopper in this store!

Be sure to stress to the manager how long you've been shopping at the store, what you like about it, and what would make it even better for you. Find out when deliveries on advertised items come in. If you're often pressed for time, you might even want to ask when the store is the least busy.

After your meeting, ask the manager to introduce you to the department managers (especially the produce, meat, grocery, deli, and bakery). For future reference, write down their names on a store directory. (Most stores have directories available for the asking. If not, you may want to do a quick sketch of the store's layout aisle by aisle.)

Store Manager Questionnaire: A Hands-On Tool

1. What is the number-one reason people shop at your store?

2. What are the best days of the week to shop here?

3. The worst?

4. What's the best time of the day to shop here?

5. What are your biggest sale items?

6. What day do your weekly sale items go on sale?

7. When are they delivered?

8. Where are your newspaper ad and circular distributed? Is there any way I can get an advance copy? Through the mail? Directly from the store?

9. Do you mail out special offers to selected customers? For what departments in the store? How can I receive them?

10. Do you have a frequent-shopper program? How do I join? What are the benefits of membership? If there is a fee to join, will you waive it for me? (Usually, if you just ask, the manager will waive the fee if he or she senses you are—or will be— a regular shopper.)

11. What are the names of your department managers (for meat, grocery, deli, bakery, seafood, dairy, customer service) and assistant managers?

12. What's the best way for shoppers to get to know you?

These are the folks you want to get to know over the next five weeks. Ask them for product literature and recipes. Even ask about upcoming product samplings (a great way to taste new products and get a coupon with a higher than normal value). Find out about special events—recipe classes, store tours, and the schedule for in-store sales and promotional events like April in Paris or Frozen Food Month. Promotions like these are usually scheduled at least twelve weeks in advance, and they usually offer above-average savings. Keep a list of the dates of each promotion and its theme—and shop accordingly. If, for example, you regularly buy frozen waffles, I guarantee you will have big savings when you stock up during your store's Frozen Food Month.

Add your name to the store's mailing list for its preferred-shopper program. Depending on the store, this program may be a state-of-the-art frequent-shopper program, a check-cashing card, a store credit card that offers bonus points, or just a simple mailing list. In any case, adding your name to the list will help you make yourself known and receive special treatment.

After the six weeks, go to a different supermarket (even though you really won't want to) and see the difference that being known really makes. You'll see how important it is to get the most out of your supermarket— and the difference it makes to your bottom line.

In Chapter 4 you'll create the single most important tool for the supermarket: your "ultimate shopping list." This list will satisfy your family, make your shopping trip faster, and save you money every time. But first, let's take a look at how a supermarket is organized and how it sells its products.

Store Layouts: Taking a Look "Behind the Shelves"

How often have you walked into a supermarket and instantly felt hungry? Maybe it was the aroma of fresh bread or the sight of case after case of dozens of freshly made deli items.

Most supermarkets have finally discovered that if the store looks and feels good to shop in, shoppers will enjoy the shopping experience, spend more time in the store, and—no surprise—buy more.

One of the most interesting supermarket chains in the country is Byerly's in Minnesota. The nine Byerly's supermarkets are carpeted and have crystal chandeliers. When shoppers and supermarket operators hear about this, their usual response is, "Carpeting? How impractical!" The management of Byerly's (and certainly I) would disagree. Shopping an hour or more in these stores is more comfortable for our legs and eyes. At this supermarket, the products are attractively presented to us, rather than just piled on the shelves.

Among my very favorite supermarkets are the Dominick's Fresh Stores in the Chicago area. As you walk in the stores, you see on your right a pizzeria, which serves pizza all day long—breakfast pizza in the morning and every style of tomato pizza the rest of the day. On your left is a coffee bar serving espresso, latte, mocha, cappuccino, and even made-to-order Italian sodas. Directly in front of you are tens of thousands of produce items in refrigerated cases and on tables decorated to look like wooden crates so the produce appears to have just arrived from the farm. Behind that, a bakery offers samples of warm bread. To the left is a full-service deli with prepared foods, fresh cheeses and provisions, and even focaccia sandwiches. I dare anyone to walk in these stores and not feel good to be there!

Understanding our senses—sight, smell, taste, touch, and hearing—is key to operating today's supermarket. Some stores are even beginning to replace their PA systems with earpiece walkie-talkies so store personnel can communicate without the harsh noise overhead that most shoppers find annoying (and that makes us want to shop faster and get out of the store).

Research has long shown that the environment in which we shop affects our spending level as well as our enjoyment. Not only do lighting and music affect our experience, so does the architectural style of the store. The landscape of supermarkets has changed. Some stores use contemporary graphics and photos to give an upscale image, while others signal low price with warehouse or backroom looks. Each style influences us differently.

Does the design of the store truly indicate the likelihood you will save money? Are no-frills operations like warehouse clubs always cheapest? Certainly not! We need to look "beyond the shelves" and at the products, pricing, and services themselves. By the same token, many stores that promote an upscale image actually offer great buys. Don't assume that just because a store looks cheap that it necessarily is.

IMPULSE BUYING: WHEN IT'S SMART AND WHEN IT'S NOT

Regardless of where you shop, every store has been designed carefully to direct your actions (and purchases). If you are aware of these "environmental motivators," you can reduce your impulse purchases and focus on the items you want. You'll also have more time to discover and, at times, sample new products.

Stores encourage impulse shopping, thereby enticing shoppers to spend more without realizing it, through the use of *integrated merchandising.* This means the store displays together items that consumers often use together—for example, beer and pretzels, or baby food and diapers—rather than arranging them by category. If you go into the produce department to buy strawberries, can you resist the pastry shells and whipped cream alongside? What about the pasta, sauce, and grated cheese displayed together at the end of an aisle? If they're all on your shopping list— or you know there's a big savings—go for it! Otherwise, you may be the next unwilling victim of impulse shopping.

Supermarkets just love shoppers who load up their carts with unplanned purchases. That's because those impulse items add a lot more dollars to our shopping tab.

Should we always skip the impulse items? No way! Discovering new products is part of the fun of supermarket shopping. The key to controlling impulse shopping is to be aware of what is an impulse buy, to decide whether you really do want the product, and to plan for the expense ahead of time.

Products that we buy on impulse are usually those that we sampled, are well displayed, or are offered at a price reduction we didn't expect. They can also entice us with strong aromas (as in the bakery department) or announcements over the PA system (as with Kmart's famous blue-light specials). Typically, our senses of sight, sound, smell, or taste take over and send our brains messages that say, "I want that!" or, "I can't live without that!"

Of course, we can well survive without these products. But there is something about impulse shopping that enriches our shopping experience and makes it more fun—almost like a reward for a shopping job well done.

It's OK to be seduced by these products—but in a controlled and planned way. First ask yourself, "Will I use this product?" As silly as it seems, most of us have bought supermarket products that are still sitting unopened in our cupboards or freezers a year later.

Also ask yourself, "Does this product replace a product already in my cart?" If it does, do a side-by-side comparison—then choose.

Next ask, "Why am I buying this?" Did you have a particularly bad or stressful day? Did you have a great day? Are you hungry? Did you just get a raise? Do you need to reward yourself? Be honest with yourself.

Finally, decide whether you really need or want it. If the answer is yes, go for it! And enjoy.

I always permit myself three impulse items. In Chapter 4, I'll tell you more about how to plan for those, when I describe how you can create your "ultimate shopping list."

SHELF SPACE

Supermarket shelves are organized not only for our convenience, but also to get us to buy certain products. Products are usually located on the shelves based on their "real estate" value. Just as an apartment building may charge a higher rental for an apartment with a better view, different product locations yield different benefits. Thus, retailers typically put their store brands at eye level or arrange them next to the higher-priced national brand for a quick no-brainer comparison. True, we can save money, but usually their motivation is that they make a bigger profit on their own label.

Companies pay the store promotional fees and allowances to get as close to consumers' eye level as possible. Think back to your own shopping experiences. Do you enjoy bending down to get that package on the bottom shelf? Have you ever taken a different product instead that was easier to reach?

Stores typically put products that have a strong following or are staples in less than desirable places. They know that regardless of where the corn flakes are on the shelf, we are still going to buy them. And the milk is way in the back of the store, forcing us to pass (and shop) thousands of other products that they would like us to buy.

TOP 10 SHELF AND DISPLAY TRICKS THAT CAN GET YOU TO SPEND MORE

One of your best tools to avoid spending more than you planned is to be aware of your supermarket's display techniques. Each supermarket (or any other store, for that matter) has its own proprietary policies and procedures for promotions and displays. However, the following tactics are among the most common:

1. Relatively high-priced items at eye level—A recent survey of shampoo products in Northern California supermarkets showed that in almost all the twenty stores visited, the highest-priced shampoos were at eye level.

2. End-of-aisle displays of products that are near their freshness expiration dates—but not on sale.

3. Displaying the most expensive children's breakfast cereals at *their* eye-level (not adults')—As you shop the aisle, you don't even realize what's causing your kids to want to put just about every cereal box imaginable in the cart.

4. Displaying candy and breakfast cereals on opposite sides in the same aisle (a parent's worst nightmare).

5. Rearranging shelves constantly—This makes us search for the regularly bought items and forces us to discover new products in the old locations.

6. Portable displays of precut (more expensive) mouth-watering fruits in produce department.

7. Massive end-of-aisle displays, large window signs showing prices, and a cluttered look—This combination creates an aura of savings that implies the store is filled with bargains.

8. Employees lavishly preparing take-home meals, right before your eyes, to create excitement and sales—This tactic is usually accompanied by offers of a free taste.

9. Items for special occasions grouped together to increase impulse sales—For example, chips, dips, and sodas may be sold near each other.

10. TVs and newspapers in the cafe seating area—This is a multi-purpose concept to get people used to staying longer in the store. (A rested shopper is a better shopper!)

As you'll discover time and time again throughout this book, preparing and sticking to your shopping list will save you the most money. Sometimes a product goes on sale unexpectedly or you discover a new product you just must have. As you prepare your shopping list, you'll leave space (and money) for those as well.

CHAPTER 2

YOUR TURN TO OUTSMART THE MARKETERS!

Today's number-one consumer complaint about the supermarket is inaccurate scanning—but whose fault is that? It turns out not to be that dreaded computer, but rather the person responsible for entering in the prices. What supermarkets must understand is that we *are* watching the prices, and a mistake of even ten cents undermines their credibility. Signs that offer the mis-scanned product free do help—but all shoppers really want is to be charged the correct price, as advertised and as labeled on the shelf. If you see a wrong price scanned at the register, don't be embarrassed or shy—speak up!

Why Should You Care?

One of the most important rules of saving money in the supermarket (or anywhere, for that matter) is to understand and believe that *it's your money*. Too many shoppers get embarrassed and don't call a cashier's attention to a mistake. That's the wrong approach to take. Fewer and fewer shoppers compare the prices featured in ads to the on-shelf prices. Is the store just doing a better job, so there are fewer mistakes? Partially, but in our everyday life the correct pricing of groceries seems not to be a top priority. It should be!

Add up the pricing mistakes, the hundreds of coupons and ad features, and count them each dollar at a time. Just use ten manufacturer coupons a week (the average coupon savings is just under sixty cents each), and you save over $300 a year. Look for store specials (they average at least a 15 percent savings), store coupons (average thirty-five cents), and special sale items. For a family of four, you can easily save another few hundred. Rebates and special coupons available from manufacturers (I'll tell you more about those in Chapter 4) can easily add up to hundreds more.

Why doesn't everyone save this much? Usually because we are either too busy (or lazy) to prepare for our supermarket trip, or we are ashamed to use coupons.

Wrong on both counts! Smart (and rich) people use coupons. With the hints and procedures you'll learn from this book, you need only minutes to prepare, and you'll save substantial dollars.

Most consumer surveys these days seem to include the finding that we shoppers aren't stupid. We know how to read labels and can tell the difference between scam and reality in the supermarket. Then why is it that each year, along with the thousands of beneficial innovations that appear on the shelves, there are also thousands of products that assume we are dense?

You know what I mean. Some products have reduced their net weight but kept their package size the same. Others have changed serving sizes to minuscule so that they can call themselves "fat-free." (The regulation is that you can call yourself fat-free if a serving contains up to ½ gram of fat.) And there's a continuous stream of products that say "no cholesterol," though they never had cholesterol to begin with. Check out Chapter 5 for a complete primer on the new labeling regulations.

HOW COLORS AFFECT OUR SUPERMARKET PURCHASES

The average package on the supermarket shelf has only about one-seventeenth of a second to attract our attention. After that, the design, color, words, and . . . oh yes

. . . the product itself have to interest us enough to put it in our cart and take it home.

Color is one of the main tools that package designers use to influence our buying decisions. Our reactions to colors are emotional rather than intellectual. According to Herb Meyers, CEO of Gerstman + Meyers, New York, one of the nation's leading package design firms, "considering that about 80 percent of consumer choices are made in store and 60 percent of those are impulse purchases, package colors can play a major role in the success or failure of a product."

On your next shopping trip, see if you react the way most shoppers do to packages that use these colors:

Red packaging (or brand names that are bold and large) makes our hearts beat faster and increases our adrenaline flow. The color communicates power and vitality and stimulates a desire to conquer.

Yellow is the most visible of all colors (which is why it is used on road signs) and makes packages look larger. According to a study by Cheskin & Masten, a research firm in Palo Alto, California, it's also the color most associated with food products. When we see yellow, we think of the sun—warmth and happiness and often "newness." Yellow is also used to convey a cut-rate price image, and, if not used properly, can detract from the perceived quality of the product.

Blue implies cleanliness and purity and induces thoughts of the sky and water. Often it conveys feelings of serenity, prestige, confidence, knowledge, and credibility (remember that the next time you have an important meeting—wear blue).

Twenty years ago, the unwritten rule about food packaging was "never use green!" The thinking was that it implied food was spoiled. Today, green is used more than most other colors and represents natural and healthy. See green and think of trees and fresh meadows. In the early 1970s packagers of "healthy" products used beige to imply natural but soon found that it washed out on the shelves. Beige was replaced with deep greens.

White makes us feel fresh and light and is often used on lower-fat and diet foods. It is associated with dairy products (milk) and hence implies the ultimate in freshness and purity.

Black is always elegant and sophisticated, and manufacturers use this color to imply a sense of class and quality for their products.

While it might seem that product packages using certain colors are trying to trick you into buying, don't worry. While a great package design can draw your attention, the product still has to stand on its own. But knowing these insider "marketing tips" can help you choose a product for the right reasons—your own.

We could follow Peter Finch's lead in the movie *Network*—open our windows and shout that we won't take it anymore. Or is it time to outsmart the marketers at their own game? It's time for a little of both. The fastest way to achieve change in the supermarket is for us to not buy a particular product—or not be fooled or misguided by a particular slogan or offer that doesn't deliver. No retailer moves faster than the supermarket—both to correct mistakes (by dropping products that we don't buy) and to capitalize on the latest consumer desires (like oat bran and fat-free).

Ten Supermarketing Tricks and How You Can Outsmart the Marketers

Here are some helpful hints that I've discovered over the years. They can help you save money and keep you from being outsmarted.

1. Love cheese? Look carefully in three places in your store for the same product—all with different prices. The dairy case usually offers staple cheeses such as cheddar, Swiss, and Monterey Jack, prepackaged at the lowest price. The deli and cheese tables may have exactly the same products, but you'll pay more. Know what you want—types of cheese, state of origin, age—and shop all three areas for the best price.

2. Does "10 Percent More Free" get you to buy extra product? Some products, beverages in particular, have packages that are larger to ensure that their production processes run at optimum speeds and have no risk of short weight (one of those things that is sure to get attention and fines from the Food and Drug Administration). These products are always giving us more than the label says, and don't think that little extra isn't built into the price. So when you

see that "extra free" label, look to see if it's the same-size package with just a limited-time special label.

3. "New and Improved" can mean the product has just come out or has been made better—or it can mean a new color, new flavor, or just a new formula. There is no word more coveted than *new* for a product on the supermarket shelf. The government knows this, so it limits use of the word on labels and packaging to just six months. But is the "New and Improved" real or just a marketing gimmick? Unfortunately this is one you probably won't be able to tell unless you can find an old package on the shelf (or in your cupboard) to compare it with. Check the ingredients and nutritional data. Look carefully for claims that are new for the product.

4. Are you buying those expensive no-fat products but gaining weight? You've switched to frozen dinners with hardly any fat and eat only no-fat cookies, but your weight hasn't changed, and you can't figure it out? You are not alone. Remember that fat, besides delivering terrific texture for a product, is also a bulking agent. Taking out the fat requires replacing it with another bulking agent. Lots of the time, it's sugar! Check out the ingredients and calorie count; you may be surprised. You might be better off just eating smaller portions of the "regular" version.

5. "Tastes great" or "improved flavor" claims always make me ask, according to whom? You should ask the same question before you switch brands and buy.

This is one of those on-pack marketing slogans that drives me nuts! If it tasted so bad before, why should I believe you now? The average package in the supermarket has about one-seventeenth of a second to attract our attention, so the manufacturer will try anything to stop us and make us look, pick up the product, and put it in our cart.

6. Healthy Choice brand started it, and everyone else followed. Now there are dozens of brands containing the word *healthy*. Under the new label regulations, new brands and products can't incorporate the word into their brand name. But the brands that were on the shelves before the regulations were enacted are "grandfathered" and can continue to use these descriptive brand names. As we scan the shelves, it therefore appears that some brands are more healthful than others. Sometimes that's true, and sometimes not. Always read both the nutritional label and the ingredients list, and judge for yourself how healthful the product is. Also check brands that use other descriptive designations that can imply a nutritional benefit. Weight Watchers' Smart Ones implies that the package contains *one* gram of fat; most do, but some of these products have two grams of fat.

7. Buy now, get something later. Most shoppers never redeem rebates or mail-in offers (in fact, less than 6 percent do). But they're a great incentive to buy a product we usually don't or to purchase multiple packages to comply with the offer. Before you put

the products in your cart, decide that you really will redeem the offer.

8. Winning a free trip to Hawaii is especially appealing in midwinter. And even though the package says in very small type that you don't have to buy the product to enter, you don't believe it. In fact, you feel that your chances just have to be a bit better if you do. Wrong! Believe it! State regulations on contests are very strict and prohibit companies from showing a preference toward purchasers. If the contest appeals to you but the product doesn't, don't buy it. Write down the entry info on a piece of paper (often there is an official entry blank near the product or by the courtesy counter) and enter. Your chances are just as good, and you haven't bought a product you'll never use.

9. Do you relax when you see a sign at the checkout that says, "We guarantee our scanner price is correct or you get the product free"? Well, don't. While systems are getting a lot better, many errors still occur at the checkout. Don't blame the cashier. The problem is with the pricing that's put in the computer. For specials, especially on the first day of a sale, bring the newspaper ad with you to the checkout and watch the register's display to make sure the scanned prices are correct.

10. Finally, here's the most important way to outsmart the marketers: Don't go shopping hungry! Our supermarkets are getting better and fresher all the time, so

when we walk in, we are bombarded with great colors, tastes, and smells. Eat first, shop later.

SELECT WHERE YOU SHOP

One of the best ways to be a great shopper is to choose a great supermarket. Easier said than done? Sometimes, but most areas now have two or three supermarkets, all competing for your food dollar. Each store may have a different positioning—low prices, high quality, personalized service, wide selection, or longer hours. First determine what is important to you, then decide whether the store meets your needs. If not, there is no way for you to have a pleasant experience.

I have developed for you a mini-audit to help you choose the best supermarket. Make one copy for each supermarket in your area. First visit and audit your regular store. Then go to the stores you have never been to or haven't shopped in for a while. This is your opportunity to find new treasures. Visit each store, complete the audit, and compare the differences.

As you review the audits, ask yourself what store made you feel the most comfortable and gave you the best savings. If you had to choose just one store to shop at for the next year, which would it be?

How to Choose the Best Supermarket for You: A Hands-On Tool

Service

1. How many store employees recognize and greet you? _____

2. Are the department managers (for meat, produce, deli, and so on) available to answer questions?
   ☐ yes ☐ no

3. Do the managers usually know the answers to your questions?
   ☐ yes ☐ no

4. How many checkers does the store use during your shopping time?   regular lanes: _____   express lanes: _____

5. Are clerks available to help you take your groceries to the car?
   ☐ yes ☐ no

6. Are rain checks for sale or out-of-stock items readily available?
   ☐ yes ☐ no

7. Can you call or fax your purchase for products advertised on sale and pick them up later?
   ☐ yes ☐ no

8. How long will the store hold them for you? _____

9. What forms of payment (in addition to cash) are accepted directly at the checkout (without requiring you to stop elsewhere in the store for approval)?
   ☐ checks ☐ credit cards ☐ debit cards

Continued on next page

10. How many express lanes are there? _____
    How many are usually open? _____

11. Does the store have frequent- or preferred-shopper programs?
    ☐ yes   ☐ no

12. Does the supermarket provide you with recipes and/or free
    samples?
    ☐ yes   ☐ no

13. Does the store deliver? Can you fax your shopping list to the
    store or place orders via phone or computer?
    ☐ yes   ☐ no

Products

1. Does the store have specialty sections that meet your needs?

Bakery	☐ yes ☐ no	Hours open: __A.M. to __P.M.
Deli	☐ yes ☐ no	Hours open: __A.M. to __P.M.
Floral	☐ yes ☐ no	Hours open: __A.M. to __P.M.
Seafood	☐ yes ☐ no	Hours open: __A.M. to __P.M.
Service meat	☐ yes ☐ no	Hours open: __A.M. to __P.M.
Video rental	☐ yes ☐ no	Hours open: __A.M. to __P.M.
Health foods	☐ yes ☐ no	
Organic foods	☐ yes ☐ no	
Special diet	☐ yes ☐ no	
Value packs	☐ yes ☐ no	
Beauty aids	☐ yes ☐ no	
In-store ATM	☐ yes ☐ no	

2. Are the products always on the shelves when you need them?
    ☐ yes   ☐ no

3. Is the store consistently out of stock on sale or advertised
    products?
    ☐ yes   ☐ no

Pricing

1. Does the store offer coupons or run sales on the products you buy most?

    ☐ yes   ☐ no

    _____ percent of your shopping list

2. If yes, how often does it run these sales?

    ☐ once a week

    ☐ once a month

    ☐ every other month

    ☐ less often

3. Does the store offer its own label or generic brands in the products that you purchase most?

    ☐ yes   ☐ no

    ___ percent of your shopping list

4. Are you satisfied with the quality of store brands?

    ☐ yes   ☐ no

5. Does the store redeem coupons from other local markets?

    ☐ yes   ☐ no

Top 10 Worst Supermarket Shopping Days

Sometimes even the best supermarkets can be a nightmare. We interviewed supermarket managers throughout the country and developed this list of the worst days to go grocery shopping. Each manager emphasized that the most pleasant shopping experience you can have is when the store is well stocked, well staffed, and ready for business. According to the managers, these are the days that "test" the system so the store may not be able to serve you properly:

1. Labor Day weekend
2. Sundays
3. Saturdays
4. Memorial Day weekend
5. Afternoons between 4 and 7 P.M.
6. Thanksgiving Eve
7. The day after a major disaster (earthquake, tornado, hurricane, snowstorm)
8. Christmas Eve
9. Fourth of July (especially if it falls on a weekend)
10. Day after Thanksgiving

CHAPTER 3

......

WHY YOU SHOULD BE A PREFERRED SHOPPER AT YOUR SUPERMARKET

For years most consumers were unaware of the electronic developments affecting supermarkets. Until very recently practically all of this technology was passive and fairly unobtrusive. Then checkout scanners appeared in almost every supermarket. Shoppers often see them as the enemy and complain about their purported inaccuracies. In the best case, however, scanners are giving America's supermarkets the tools they need to provide us with instant savings and preferred shopping benefits. Think of these benefits as holding a supermarket's gold or platinum card "with all the privileges"! As the credit card companies offer special services, so does the supermarket.

Just about all the supermarket operators I've spoken to have either instituted a preferred-shopper (frequent-) program or are investigating one for their store. The reason? The programs combine the motivation of the airline frequent-flier programs with the success of in-supermarket coupons at checkout to create an effective relationship-building tool every supermarket wants.

And can you blame them? What supermarket wouldn't want a loyal shopper who shops only at their store? Today, most consumers shop at three different supermarkets each month.

According to the May 1995 issue of *Supermarket Business* magazine, electronic marketing programs emerged in the mid-1980s in response to changing consumer demographics and media delivery systems. In the article, Jeanne Whalen quotes a Food Marketing Institute (FMI) study reporting that by year-end more than 60 percent of food retailers would have a frequent-shopper program in place. The FMI also found that grocery chains credited these programs for sales increases of 10 to 20 percent a year.

A drawback for the occasional store shopper is that retailers are moving toward targeting their best, most loyal customers with better-than-before specials and discounts. One store owner (who didn't want to be identified) said he no longer mails coupons or sale circulars to customers who are not enrolled in his frequent-shopper program.

Types of Preferred-Shopper Programs

Preferred-shopper programs come in many shapes and sizes, and it pays to shop around for the best one. Joe Wood, marketing manager at Roundy's Supermarkets of Wisconsin, has developed one of the best programs in the country by understanding his shoppers' needs—not just letting technology force a program down their throats. Joe's philosophy led to the success of his program: "To be truly effective, a frequent-shopper program must be developed with the consumers' benefits in mind. It must provide the retailer with a means of identifying who his best customers are and allow him to reward them. And lastly, a frequent-shopper program cannot serve as a substitute for a clean store with friendly, courteous employees."

Frequent-Shopper Programs

A *frequent-shopper program* gives added value to customers who regularly shop in a certain store or buy certain products. Typically the store issues membership cards, which it uses to track purchases. Usually the shopper accumulates points or the store uses a historical record of product purchase as the basis for reward redemption. The points or dollar values are credited electronically to consumer accounts, much as an airline frequent-flier program keeps track of mileage. The consumer later exchanges the points or dollars for awards such as discounts on the total purchase, or discounts or free products in a specific department or on specific items. Some programs use only one of these; some incorporate all of them.

One frequent-shopper option you really need to check out is whether your store's program varies the points or dollar incentive accumulations by offering bonus points on specific items or departments. (This is similar to double- or triple-mileage bonuses for specific car rentals or special city-to-city flights.) For example, a frequent-shopper program could be set up to give bonus points on deli purchases only to people who have not shopped in the deli. The idea is to encourage them to try shopping in that section of the store. Preferred regular shoppers of the deli department could be awarded bonus points when and if they maintain a certain amount of purchases from that department.

Keep in mind that these programs will ask (and most will record) your shopping preferences and demographics. The more you tell about you and your family, the more targeted the offers—especially on the products that you are not buying but they would like you to.

Front-End Electronic Marketing

Other stores use *front-end electronic marketing*—electronically based programs in which consumers receive rewards based on the number and value of their shopping trips and/or purchases. These are similar to frequent-flier or credit card–based programs that accumulate points based on purchases. The cashier scans your card or keys your membership number into the system. Many retailers build in different reward levels to acknowledge shoppers with higher-than-average spending. These rewards can be in the form of discounts, free products, prizes, or services. As more stores' computer programs become more sophisticated, front-end electronic marketing will be offered more as a part of a preferred-shopper program than as a stand-alone offering.

Purchase-Triggered or Purchase-Activated Coupon Programs

To encourage store loyalty, many stores use *purchase-triggered* or *purchase-activated* coupon programs. The store issues its customers coupons or other incentives to return to that particular store. For example, coupon machines at checkout counters distribute one to three coupons at the time of sale. These coupons can be redeemed only at that store.

These programs give customers incentives without recording their identity or storing data about their shopping trends. The coupons are for saving on future shopping trips, cash rebates, or for goods and services at noncompeting retailers. These coupons are "triggered" by specific purchases at the register.

The coupons fall into three categories. The most common category is coupons issued by a competing brand. The maker of that brand has paid the coupon company a fee to ensure that you receive a higher-than-normal face value coupon for its product when you buy a competing product. The second category of coupon is for a larger size of a product that you are buying. The maker of the product pays a fee to have these coupons issued in order to increase your usage (and its sales). Less often, you may receive a coupon for complimentary products. Here, the coupon you receive is for a product that you aren't buying (on this shopping trip) but that has historically been purchased by most shoppers at the same time as some other product you are buying (for example, a coupon for peanut butter when you buy jelly).

Instant Electronic Discounts

Stores that use *instant electronic discounts* automatically subtract cash discounts from customers' orders when customers give cards to cashiers (who then scan them) and purchase specific products. To identify these products to customers ahead of time, the store may use mailers, flyers, or "shelf talkers" (signs on shelves near the products reminding customers of the savings). These discounts are sometimes called "paperless coupons." As our use of supermarket computers becomes more sophisticated, electronic discounts (using debit cards, credit cards, or preferred-shopper cards) are expanding to include discounts on local services and restaurants.

Supermarkets are also offering shoppers contests (with prizes as glamorous as trips to Hawaii), free long-distance calling, and other nontraditional rewards. The coupons, rebates, and other offers almost always vary from visit to visit, as they are all sponsored (paid for) by a manufacturer, and the coupon is triggered by a particular size, brand, flavor, or quantity that you are buying. These programs will continue to expand and become commonplace. Look for retailer point programs to sire catalogs reminiscent of the once-prevalent Green Stamp programs of the fifties and sixties.

WHAT MAKES PREFERRED-SHOPPER PROGRAMS BENEFICIAL?

We asked retailers with preferred-shopper programs what makes them beneficial to consumers. Their answers—as well as recently published articles about the programs—usually focused on or involved consumer savings.

Greg Gregerson, president of Gregerson's Foods of Alabama, strongly believes in his frequent-shopper club, aptly named Club Greg. He has eliminated practically all other forms of advertising and promotion. "Club Greg is a beneficial way for us to reward our best customers. We couldn't do this before because we lacked the technology. It's a way to say thank you to our customers." After I had spent time with Gregerson, feeling his commitment to serve his shoppers with real value and looking over six months of mailings with free-product coupons, I wanted to move to Birmingham, Alabama, just to become a member myself!

Steve Boone, president and CEO of Beverages & More, a beverage retailer, stated that its Club Bev card provides consumers with additional discounts on the store's already low prices.

In some programs consumers not only save at grocery stores but at other retailers in their area. Albert Lees of Lees' Grocery in Westport, Massachusetts, believes that customers who belong to frequent-shopper programs are a part of a "large subset with small benefits." When a customer enrolls in their program, he or she has access to discounts from a number of other local vendors, including dry cleaners and museums.

Programs that offer discounts from other organizations are called "affinity programs." Today they are not yet a part of all frequent-shopper programs. But look for them to expand and become more widespread.

According to the Food Marketing Institute, the most prevalent benefits of frequent-shopper or preferred-shopper programs are:

- Free merchandise or hot coupons (50 percent off products) on the initial signup for the program
- Electronic discounts or paperless coupons
- Continuity or "point" programs (for instance, if you accumulate 1,000 points, you get a gift certificate for $10 off your next purchase or free merchandise)
- Association programs—generally charitable contributions tied to dollars spent
- Sweepstakes and drawings (such as $50 gift certificates, manufacturer-sponsored vacations)
- Affinity programs with local vendors (for example, discounts with card at area establishments such as dry cleaners and auto service dealers)

- "Gold Member" benefits awarded to best customers only (usually including targeted mailings with newsletter and coupons, free delivery of groceries, new-product sampling, private shopping hours, a "convenience certificate" allowing the member to select any item and "put it on sale," and a Birthday Club or Kids' Club)

PRIVACY CONSIDERATIONS: TEN QUESTIONS YOU NEED TO ASK BEFORE SIGNING UP

The major drawback to these programs, according to industry experts, centers around issues of privacy and confidentiality. Greg Gregerson of Gregerson's Foods believes that consumers in his store's program are very concerned with privacy issues. Club Greg guarantees its members that it will not sell customer demographic information—be it addresses, phone numbers, or consumer shopping habits—to outside groups, including telemarketers. Today Club Greg members account for over 80 percent of all the supermarket's transactions. Every six to eight weeks, club members get a mailing that includes advance notices of specials, special coupons, and free products.

As frequent-shopper programs are coming on strong, some consumers are skeptical. Our weekly Supermarket Checkout Chat on America On-Line explored this issue, and most shoppers were cautious. Steve Levinthal, a computer consultant and writer who is one of our regulars, offers his personal shopping experience: "I do use my preferred card, but I know I'm not sure I'm getting any extra savings [that] I wouldn't have gotten otherwise. My concern is that they're just using it for marketing info to track what I am buying."

As we get more and more computerized and data-based, it is essential that each of us ask the right questions before signing up for any program. Supermarkets, likewise, need to develop (and publish) a specific privacy policy statement covering in-house use of data and the release of any personalized data to outside parties. In the meantime, before you sign up, ask these ten questions:

1. *Consent*—Does the store ask you to sign a waiver allowing it to collect personalized shopping information?

2. *Behavior*—What kind of information is asked about you and your shopping habits? How will this information be used?

3. *Ownership*—Who owns the data? Make sure that any application you sign clearly states who owns the data and whether the data may be transferred or sold to others.

4. *Disclosure*—Will the use of personalized data, either in-house or by outside parties, be disclosed?

5. *Removal of names*—Are members offered the opportunity to have their names removed from the database if they desire?

6. *Data transfer*—Must the consumer consent before data may be transferred (rented, sold, or exchanged) to outside parties?

7. *Data content*—Will the information collected be reviewed to limit its content to the necessity of the application, and will it be used exclusively for the purposes outlined to the consumer?

8. *Accuracy*—What are the procedures to ensure that all personalized data are accurate, up to date, and retained no longer than required for the purposes intended?

9. *Consumer access*—Do members have access to their personalized information, and will they have a chance to correct any information if necessary?

10. *Security*—What procedures are in place to prevent unauthorized access, alteration, or release of personalized information?

If you aren't satisfied with the answers to any of these questions, don't sign up!

CHAPTER 4

···

VALUE: THE NUMBER-ONE GOAL

The question consumers most often ask me is, How can I save *more* money in my supermarket?

Most of us are good shoppers. We clip coupons occasionally, if not regularly, use some store brands, and look out for specials. We recognize that there is a gold mine in savings out there—but we're not quite sure how to save the most possible.

I've learned that the best way to be a *smart* shopper is to focus on value, not just on price. As I shared with you earlier, my goal is for supermarkets to help us achieve value by balancing quality, products, service—and, of course, price.

This chapter will give you the ideas and hints you want, to help you save as much money and get as much value as you can. Let's take a look at the tools that practically guarantee saving big bucks: a well-planned shopping list and coupons.

TEN STEPS TO CREATE A SHOPPING LIST THAT SAVES YOU MONEY

Practically every shopper that I've ever interviewed agrees that a shopping list is important. Then why don't we do it? Most of us complain that it takes too much time to create or plan, or that we can't think about our shopping trip while still at home. Some shoppers have even told me that making a list is just a waste of their time and that it's one of those boring tasks to avoid. Well, all that stops right here! From now on, your shopping list is going to be fun and easy, and it will save you lots of money.

Most supermarkets today are scanning at the checkout, so each week your register receipt is a detailed list of what items you bought, what prices you paid, and the value of the coupons you used. This register receipt is the foundation for my "ultimate shopping list." If you are like most shoppers, each week 80 percent of the products you buy are similar to what you bought the week before. Put aside your shopping lists for parties or holiday meals when you have the entire family over; our focus is on your everyday family shopping.

I've taken the best of all the ideas I've seen, heard, and tested to create my *ultimate shopping list.* This approach will take you a bit more time than you are used to—but only at first. I guarantee that after you have used this method a few times, you'll never stop using it. It's an easy ten-step method:

```
 1 @ 2/3.00
      SMART ONES       1.50
 1 @ 2/3.00
      SMART ONES       1.50
      HEALTHY CHC      2.49
      CHICK FAJITA     2.49
      GRDN BURGER      3.29
      PIZZA            2.19
      PIZZA            2.19
      SARA LEE         2.49
      RICE CAKES       2.29
      RICE CAKES       2.29
 1 @ 2/5.00
      PAPER TOWEL      2.50 T
 1 @ 2/5.00
      PAPER TOWEL      2.50 T
 1 @ 2/5.00
      PAPER TOWEL      2.50 T
      SALAD MIX        2.49
      EGGO WAFFLES     1.99
      HELTHY CHOIC     2.49
      HEALTY CHOIC     2.49
      CHKN BREASTS     2.39
      B&J YOGURT       2.89
      HANNA MULTI      2.59
      MILK 1-11        1.48
      O/R POPCORN      3.43
 1 @ 4/5.00
      WELCH CONC       1.25
 1 @ 4/5.00
      WELCH CONC       1.25
      TRIDENT           .89
      TRIDENT           .89
      PAR AUTO         2.33 T
      DANNON YOGRT      .75
      MAZOLA OIL       2.39
      SALAD MIX        2.49
      CELLO CARROT     1.19
      DANNON YOGRT      .75
      PASTA SAUCE      1.21
      PARMSAN GRAT     1.49
      WHEAT GERM       3.95
      K MINI WHTS      4.45
      FIGURINES        1.99
 1 @ 2/1.00
      CHILI MIX         .50
      QUICK OATS       1.59
```

1. Take the detailed register receipt of a typical week's shopping, and tape it on an 8½" x 11" piece of white paper. Place the register tape along the left side of the paper, leaving a ¾-inch margin. If your register receipt exceeds 11 inches long, cut it carefully and tape the rest of it on additional pieces of paper.

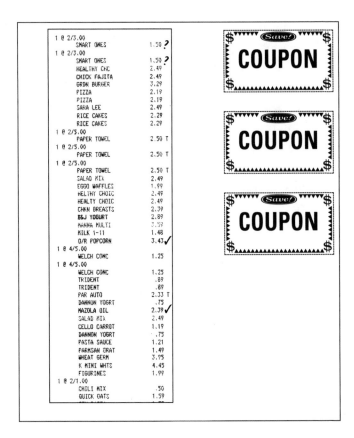

2. Go to your coupon and rebate file (more on that later in this chapter), and with a pencil, put a check mark right on the receipt alongside every *brand name* that you have collected a coupon or rebate for. If you have a coupon for another brand but the same type of product, put a question mark alongside the register listing.

3. Add up the total value of all coupons and rebates. Place all in an envelope marked with the number of coupons and total value. For example, write, "20 coupons & rebates = $17.30."

4. Review the current newspaper ads and store circulars for your supermarket. If you shop more than one store, do it for each. Put a $ to the left of every product on your receipt that is on sale. As you did with your coupons, also mark like items (those that you would consider to replace your normal brand). Mark these with a $ in a circle. Also look for any store coupons in the ad, and mark as you did for manufacturer coupons in step 2.

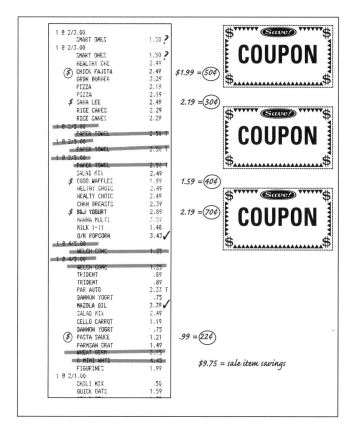

5. To the right of each item on sale, write down the sale price. Subtract the sale price from the price you last paid, and write down the savings. Circle it. Add up all the savings on both $ and Ⓢ. On the same envelope, under your coupon savings, write down the total amount, for example, "sale items savings = $9.75."

6. Compare your list against your inventory in your kitchen, refrigerator, freezer, and pantry. Cross out any item that does not have a √, ?, $, or Ⓢ next to it or that you already have enough of on hand to last till your next shopping trip.

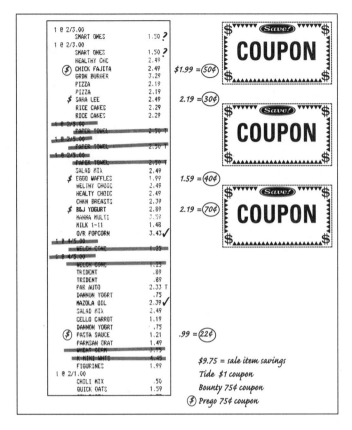

7. Next, go through your coupon file to see if you have any high-value coupons for any products that you regularly use or would like to try. (Limit yourself to no more than five new or never-before-tried products.) Add those to the bottom of the list. List them by brand name, and mark them with √,?, $, or ⑤, if applicable. Add any savings on these items to the outside of your envelope. For this example, let's use $2.50.

20 coupons & rebates = $17.30
sale items savings = $9.75
extra coupons = $2.50
$29.55

8. You're now ready to go shopping. Total the amount on the outside of your envelope. Our example totals $29.55— circle it! Check to verify that all the coupons and rebates you selected are inside the envelope and you have the shopping list you just created with all the markings. Before you enter the store, take a look at the outside of the envelope marked with your savings, and remember the amount. This is the minimum amount to save on this trip. Set your objective to beat this total before you even walk into the store.

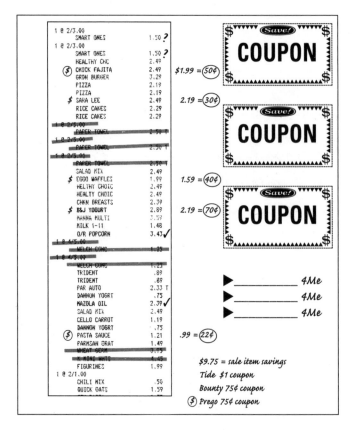

9. For me a big part of enjoying the supermarket is finding new products. Whether at an in-store sampling (be sure to ask for a coupon) or just on the shelf, I can't resist buying something not on my list. I always permit myself *three* impulse items. These are products that I didn't even think about before I walked in the store. Choose your own limit—you may want to have one impulse product for each member of your family, or one as a reward for anyone who shops with you. Whatever the quantity, the

important rule is that you set a limit before you go in the store, and that you write down the name and price of the product as you select it on your list. Put down a fun designation alongside. I use "4ME."

10. When you get home, compare the results—the bottom line—of this week's shopping trip to last week's. How much more did you save? File your shopping lists in a three-ring binder, and keep track of your weekly savings. You can also use these lists to compare the seasonal pricing of products and special events. For example, many supermarkets have events that include Canned Foods Sales or Frozen Food Festivals with substantial savings and high-value coupons. Make a note of these, and use these events and specials to stock up.

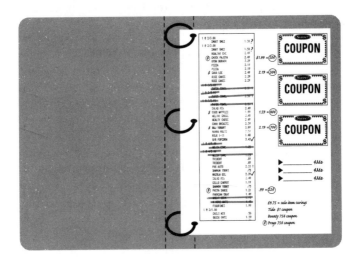

Use my "ultimate shopping list" every trip, and I promise you will save money!

Coupons Really Do Save Us Money: Five Simple Strategies

You've seen the headlines on those supermarket tabloids that declare how some shoppers buy a hundred dollars of groceries for a fraction of that amount. A guest on *Oprah*, Tom Lemke, explained how he was able to buy over $400 of groceries for under $120. While these extraordinary savings are possible, they usually don't occur on our regular weekly shopping trips. A good measure of coupon success is 15 percent of your total bill. For the average family of four, that can easily translate to a yearly savings of over $700!

How Coupons Work

Manufacturers and supermarkets want us to redeem their coupons. Couponing is a proven marketing tool that can not only build sales but also convert shoppers to a particular brand. During new-product introductions, high-value coupons are often offered initially, then values drop as sales increase. Products such as cereals, for which brand loyalty is lower than average (and the profit margin higher), offer the highest-value coupons.

There are basically two types of coupons: manufacturer and retailer. Manufacturer coupons usually appear in newspapers, freestanding inserts (full-color supplements), direct-mail pieces, and magazines. The manufacturer pays the store each redeemed coupon's face value, plus a handling charge. Retailer coupons are redeemed directly by the supermarket. Often the manufacturer has paid the retailer a promotional allowance to compensate for the expense.

In supermarkets that promote double or triple couponing, usually only manufacturer coupons are eligible. Most stores also limit such offers to coupons of up to a certain face value.

Making Coupons Work for You

How can you save $700 or more each year by using coupons? Just follow these five simple strategies, and you'll immediately increase your coupon savings:

1. *Collect coupons from as many sources as possible.* You'll find coupons just about everywhere you look: in your newspaper, in newspaper supplements, in magazines, in your mailbox, from mail-in rebates, at in-store samplings, in circulars, on pads attached to supermarket shelves, through on-line services (Prodigy and CompuServe, so far), and in coupon dispensers. As of this writing, the latest estimate for 1995 was that over 400 billion coupons would be distributed. Get your fair share!

2. *Discard any coupons you know you will never use.* If it's the wrong product, wrong flavor, or for whatever reason, if you are not going to buy the product, throw out the coupon. Check the expiration date on the coupon as well. If you don't expect to redeem it by that date, throw it out. By the way, Nielsen Coupon Clearing House reports that 96 percent of coupons are

never used. Don't feel guilty discarding coupons—the object is to save money on the type of products you want and use.

3. *Keep your coupons organized.* Don't just throw coupons in a drawer. Divide them by product type (cereals, frozen dinners, salad dressing, etc.) and then put them in order of descending value—the highest-value coupons in front. Then note the expiration date and put those expiring soonest up front. Put those with no expiration date last.

4. *Experiment with new brands and new products.* This is one of the best ways to find those hidden treasures. Most supermarkets insist that a company distribute high-value coupons when it introduces a new product.

5. *Combine offers to save even more.* The ultimate way to save is to wait for the supermarket to feature a special price, use your coupon, mail in proof of purchase for a rebate, and shop on specially advertised discount value days. It doesn't come together all that often, and it's hard work. But if you start thinking about combining offers, you'll find you can often combine at least two for many products.

As an experiment, save this week's supermarket receipt. Spend the next month preparing for and following these five strategies. Then when you've collected your coupons and checked the advertised specials, take a copy of the original receipt and buy the same products. Be open to new brands (including store brands) or new package sizes. You'll be surprised how much you'll have saved.

DON'T FORGET THOSE REBATES

Refunds and rebate offers usually take one of three forms:
1. A direct cash or check rebate on a purchase
2. A coupon to be used on a future purchase
3. A product sample delivered to your home

Manufacturers offer rebates or refunds for the same reasons they provide coupons, with one big difference. While the average value of coupons is over fifty cents, the cash value of refunds is almost always at least twice as much. And there's a good reason for that. Usually you will have to add your own postage and supply your own envelope for mailing. That means that right off the bat, you've spent close to forty cents, so make sure that your rebate savings are at least twice that, or don't even bother.

The rebate process—from your mailing to your receipt of cash, coupon, or sample—usually takes from four to eight weeks. Look carefully at the fine print in the offer. By law, the offer will specify the processing time.

Sending for a rebate can take a lot of work. Most times you have to save just about everything from the package and sales receipt. The most common (80 percent) of on-package requirements requested are proof-of-purchase seals (POPS) and universal product code seals (UPCS). POPS are sections of packages containing the words "proof of purchase." UPCS are the vertical stripes (usually in a 1" × 1½" white area, with numbers below) that are scanned at the checkout to record pricing. They are commonly known as bar codes.

Practically all rebates require a copy of your original cash register receipt. While it might seem that the manufacturer doesn't trust you, that's not necessarily the reasoning. The manufacturer uses the receipt to verify the store location and the retail selling price of the product. The manufacturer wants to make sure that if it spends money on a promotion, the supermarket passes the savings on to consumers, rather than keeping an added profit.

Some manufacturers may also request net weight statements, size designations, product names, box tops or bottoms, ingredients lists, tear strips, labels, or cap liners. Just in case, save the entire package until you send in your rebate request.

Where are you most likely to find rebate offers? Start by looking in these places:

- In the supermarket at the customer-service counter, on bulletin boards, on the shelves, and on special end-aisle displays. Also, ask department managers.
- Newspapers and magazines often contain rebate offers. Look in the newspaper's food section as well as in the coupon inserts.
- Refund forms are plentiful in direct-mail coupon books and value packs.
- The manufacturers themselves are a terrific source of high-value rebate forms. Just call up the toll-free customer-service line listed on the package, and see what they have to offer. Remember that rebate offers will change, so call often. Ask if the compa-

ny has a rebate mailing list that your name and address can be added to.

To use rebates and refunds, follow the same rules as you would for your coupons:

- Use them to save money on the products you use or to try a new product.
- Don't clutter up your drawers or coupon file with those you'll never use.
- Organize offers by brand name, and keep all cash register tapes easily accessible.
- Within each product category, file according to expiration date.

WHAT IF YOU HATE USING COUPONS? THE FIVE-STEP/FIVE-MINUTE SHOPPING LIST

You don't want to use coupons? I hope by now I've convinced you that they are easy to use—and if you don't use them, well, you're just throwing away money. But if you still don't want to use them, you can save money by being organized and doing a bit of planning. I promise it will take only five minutes at home and will shorten your in-store shopping time. Here's what to do:

1. Prepare your shopping list. The first time you do this will be a bit harder and less organized. Later in these

steps, you'll shop a bit differently so that your list takes less time to prepare. On your register receipt from last week's shopping trip, cross off all the items you don't need. Spend a few minutes and do a quick check in the freezer, fridge, and cupboard to make sure you are not duplicating any products you already have.

2. At the bottom of the list, add any other items you know you need.

3. Under your additional items, draw one horizontal line for each of your "allowed" impulse items. Keep the number of impulse items fixed from week to week—don't vary it. That just wastes time and money!

4. Shop the store in a logical pattern. Start from either the front or the back and shop the whole store, aisle by aisle. While this may seem like a waste of time (when you know you don't need anything down a particular aisle), it's an important tool to saving money. As you are shopping, look at the shelf signs! Most supermarkets have clearly marked (usually in yellow or red) "shelf talkers" that identify products on sale and their cost savings. In addition, many stores have installed coupon dispensers, some with a flashing light. While these do clutter up the aisle, they are a great source of coupons. (I know that you refuse to use coupons, but what if they are staring you in the face? These are pretty painless—no preparation, no clipping.) Check them out, and remember that the coupons offered usually change weekly.

5. One of the biggest time savers in shopping is to prepare your list in the (almost) exact layout of the store.

For example, if you enter your store in the produce aisle, your shopping list should read in the order that the products appear on the shelf, and so on for each aisle and product.

This kind of list usually takes a lot of time to prepare, so I'll give you one of my personal favorite tips to try for yourself: This will work only if you are careful with the way you position products in your cart. Place the products in your cart in the order of the store. At the checkout remove them in the reverse order (last in, first out). Make sure you place them on the checkout belt in order— don't just pile them one on top of each other. Your register receipt (for your next shopping trip) will then follow the store's layout, in reverse order the first week, and alternating each week. It's a guaranteed time saver.

USING CREDIT CARDS TO SAVE MONEY AT THE SUPERMARKET

As credit cards have become accepted by more and more supermarkets throughout the country, they also join the ranks of the most effective ways shoppers can increase the value of their supermarket shopping trip.

A Yankelovich Partners survey sheds some light on why more and more consumers are using their credit cards at the supermarket. According to the survey, supermarket shoppers who pay for their groceries with credit cards use these cards because "they worry about carrying too much cash around" (73 percent) and "they don't like to carry a checkbook" (62 percent). One-third of the supermarket users said they choose to use certain supermarkets because they accept credit cards.

The survey also reports that supermarket credit card users are much more likely to pay their credit card bills in full each month than those who don't use their cards in supermarkets. (Specifically, 72 percent of supermarket users pay off their balance versus 45 percent of non-supermarket users.) A surprising finding uncovered by an American Express survey was that 69 percent of consumers felt that offering a variety of payment options was more important when choosing a supermarket than coupons, special discounts, and frequent-buyer programs.

In addition to the convenience and time savings at the register, some other reasons to consider using your credit card at the supermarket are as follows:

- You can stock up on products that are on an unexpected "super sale."
- Your receipts provide a record of purchase for budgeting and tax purposes.
- You can keep money in the bank, earning interest, until you pay your bill each month.
- The regular monthly billing cycle can help you manage your cash flow.
- In some cases, you can earn points on your frequent-flier program or supermarket co-branded card.

On January 19, 1995, MasterCard, in conjunction with NatWest Bank and Penn Traffic Supermarkets, launched the first co-branded credit card to offer consumers an unlimited 2 percent rebate toward groceries on all purchases made with the card. "The average family of four can save more than $100 annually by using the Penn Traffic MasterCard," said Kristine Crow, senior vice president of co-branded and affinity marketing for Penn Traffic. She explained that the average annual grocery expenditure by a family of four is $4,732, according to the Food Marketing Institute.

Based on the successful introduction of this program, look for more supermarkets to follow with their own co-branded credit cards (some will probably be combined with their frequent-shopper programs to offer even more benefits). Ask at your store's courtesy counter if such a credit card program exists. If it does, find out if there are any annual charges or fees. If you are a regular shopper at the store—or intend to be—ask if the fee can be waived for you.

On-Line Supermarket Shopping Strategies

The supermarket is one of the last retail environments to take advantage of the new technologies. Is it because the very primal act of food gathering is at odds with science? Or because our shopping experience should focus on tastes, aromas, and freshness rather than high-speed efficiencies?

I remember watching *The Jetsons* with awe; maybe you did too! Food shopping and preparation were instantaneous—as easy as speaking into a speakerphone. George and Judy's words became foods that appeared in seconds, cooked and on the plate, ready to eat. Elroy (to his mother's dismay) was never at a loss for a quick snack.

Today, we are closer to that convenience than you might think. Courtesy of Peapod and Shoppers Express, two on-line supermarket home-shopping services, millions of Americans can now shop from the convenience and privacy of home.

Is supermarket shopping by computer right for you? If you want to save time, have a standard shopping list from week to week, or just can't get out of the house, on-line food shopping may be your answer. One of the biggest pluses of shopping on-line so far is that both Peapod and Shoppers Express are services partnered with neighborhood supermarkets.

According to Debra Lambert, spokesperson for Safeway's Northern California division (a Peapod retailer), "It's easy to do. It's convenient. It's logical. It shows customers what the specials are, and it sorts by value. It's a very simple program to use." Diane Maffia, consumer affairs manager at Jewel in Chicago, another Peapod retailer, offers an additional consumer benefit in shopping for those who are able to use (and have) a computer: "It reaches customers who up to now couldn't physically go to the grocery store, such as the homebound and elderly." Many seniors are becoming computer literate through training and services from organizations such as SeniorNet (available through America On-Line), which have also set up locations in downtown areas where those without their own computers can use one for a small fee.

Another benefit of on-line food shopping is the ease of price comparisons. On both services, products are listed in department order, so the on-shelf and display confusion doesn't exist. For staple items, on-line shopping is therefore an easy and fast way to compare prices and decide which brand to buy.

Both Peapod and Shoppers Express understand that we might be a bit reluctant to turn over our shopping to someone else—especially when it comes to fresh foods. They both offer satisfaction guarantees, take coupons, and feature weekly and super specials right on your computer screen.

Unfortunately neither service is available nationwide, but both are growing rapidly. The following sections describe each service and provide the number to call to see if they are servicing your area. If they are not as of yet, don't worry. At the rate they are growing, they probably will be soon.

Peapod

Peapod prides itself on personalized service. Each order is handpicked right in a supermarket by trained Peapod shoppers, who are rewarded with cash for a perfect shopping record. They are taught how to pick the best meats, produce, and fresh foods. On Peapod, you can order your groceries and drugstore items from home or work using your computer, fax, or phone. Peapod, based in Evanston, Illinois, currently serves more than 8,500 households in

Chicago's North Side and suburbs and parts of Northern California.

To get started with Peapod, you need to choose between ordering by computer or by phone/fax. The computer starter kit includes Peapod's software. The phone/fax starter kit includes the Jewel item catalog. Each starter kit is $29.95. In addition, Peapod charges a monthly fee of $4.95. This fee covers unlimited on-line shopping time, software upgrades, technical support, and other services.

You can shop anytime day or night by computer or fax, or during regular business hours by phone. Peapod delivers during a scheduled (by you) ninety-minute "window" Tuesday through Sunday. You can pay for your groceries by check, credit card, or Peapod electronic payment. Coupons are redeemed. Peapod charges $6.95 per order, plus 5 percent of your total order. For example, if you order $100 worth of merchandise, your fee would be $11.95 for delivery.

To order the Peapod starter kit or check on availability in your area, call (847) 864-8900.

Shoppers Express

Shoppers Express Inc., headquartered in Bethesda, Maryland, is the nation's fastest-growing provider of home-shopping services to supermarkets, drugstores, and mass merchant retailers, including the Kroger Company, Safeway Stores, Giant Foods, Winn-Dixie, Foodtown, Quality Food Centers, First National Supermarkets, Harmons, Farm Fare, and the Vons Companies.

Customers can place their orders by phone or fax and through America On-Line (AOL). The orders are transmitted to the fulfillment store nearest the customer in aisle sequence for selection. The order is picked by trained store personnel and then delivered by Shoppers Express, using special thermal containers, in two convenient shifts as late as 9:30 P.M. The delivery fee varies throughout the country, depending on area, from $5.00 to $11.95 per order with no additional fees. They do offer a senior citizen discount on the delivery charge in most areas. Regular AOL on-line membership fees and charges apply. Checks and credit cards are accepted. Coupons are redeemed.

To find out if Shoppers Express is available in your area, or if you are not an America On-Line subscriber, call (800) 827-3338 for ten hours of free trial membership.

TOP 10 SUPERMARKET VALUE TIPS

This chapter gives you the most ways to save money on your supermarket shopping trip and the most information to remember. I'm sure you'll find that this section of the book will become one of your most used references to get started. Once you've put these tools into practice, they will become second nature. But until then, here's a recap of the most important tips:

1. Always prepare your shopping list beforehand. Follow the format illustrated for my "ultimate shopping list" earlier in this chapter for maximum savings and time efficiency.

2. Always use coupons—never go shopping without them. Set your coupon savings goal for at least 15 percent of your total bill.

3. Never shop when hungry or rushed. Leave the kids (or your spouse) at home if they are tired, cranky, or just don't want to shop.

4. Experiment with store brands. Look for shelf tags saying, "Compare to national brands and save," but keep in mind that you should always check the ingredients, nutritional information, and size of package to make sure you are choosing a like item.

5. Use your credit card to receive bonus points or to stock up on unexpected sale items—but only if you'll use them within three months or before their expiration date.

6. Look for value packs or larger sizes that offer a discounted price per ounce. Always look at the on-shelf and in-store signs that offer price savings. It's the best way to find value that you might have missed.

7. Buy no more than three impulse items not on your shopping list. You can always buy more on your next trip.

8. Shop the entire store. With store layouts today, you may well find different products in different sizes in different parts of the store.

9. Always ask the department managers and courtesy counter for any coupons or rebates they may have. Don't rely on just those posted on the bulletin board, but check there, too!

10. Shop only at a supermarket that you enjoy.

SHOPPING FOR SINGLES WITHOUT SPENDING MORE

How many times have you bought a product at the supermarket, knowing the package was too big? You knew you would wind up wasting some of the product. You knew you were wasting money, and you just wished a smaller size were available.

Or maybe you did find the perfect size for your family of one or two, but the price was so high that you calculated it would be less expensive to buy the bigger size and throw out the rest before the expiration date. Often those products "for one" sound great . . . until you look at the price.

The average American family just isn't average anymore. According to the Bureau of Labor Statistics, the fastest-growing segment of the population is divorced parents with one child—a family of two. More and more singles, both young and old, are shopping for themselves and face higher unit prices for smaller sizes.

Let's do a quick comparison of some recent national averages of retail supermarket sizes and prices. Be sure to notice the price per ounce in each case:

Quaker instant oatmeal

18-oz. box	$2.45	13.6¢/oz.
42-oz. box	$3.69	8.8¢/oz.

Starkist chunk light tuna in water

pack of 3 3-oz. cans	$2.25	25¢/oz.
9-oz. can	$1.49	16.6¢/oz.

Tombstone pizza—pepperoni and sausage

Tombstone for One

(7.05 oz.)	$2.19	31.1¢/oz.
Tombstone (22 oz.)	$3.49	15.9¢/oz.

Kellogg's cereals

Kellogg's Fun Pack

(6 boxes)	$3.25	50.8¢/oz.

Kellogg's Variety Pack

(10 boxes)	$4.49	42.8¢/oz.

The manufacturers seem to be assuming that if we have a smaller family unit, we have more money.

No one would argue that it costs more to package smaller sizes, but this much more? So what can smaller family units do? Just grin and bear it? Write and complain? Just accept the price discrimination? No, there are other options.

Remember that lots of foods in the supermarket service departments are sold by the pound. The fresh meat, seafood, deli, produce, and bakery are perfect places to buy the exact sizes you need without paying any more than if you had a family of six. For convenience, the deli now offers more prepared foods than ever before, so if you want one burrito, one slice of pizza, and 2 ounces of antipasto, you can get them—and all priced by the pound.

The bulk foods section of the store also allows you to buy exact amounts. It might be the best place to buy cereal or oatmeal for occasional use.

Check out the private label—the store's own brand—for grocery items like tuna. Often the store brand not only offers a price savings, but is packaged in different sizes. To do a fair comparison, be sure to check out the unit price label on the shelf, as well as the ingredients list and Nutritional Facts label.

Buying for one or a small family doesn't have to be more expensive. You just have to plan your meals around the tens of thousands of products that are available the way you want to buy them.

BUYING FOOD ELSEWHERE: BIG SAVINGS OR BIG HASSLE?

The average supermarket occupies 35,000 square feet and has about 35,000 products on its shelves. To some retailers, this isn't quite big enough—much to the dismay of some consumers.

Building bigger supermarkets is nothing new. Thirty years ago, as a teenager in New Jersey, I would join my parents on an excursion to the Grand Way on Route 17 in Paramus. Grand Union built this store based on the *hypermarché* model in France. This store was approximately 75,000 square feet and sold just about everything you could want—clothing, hardware, appliances, and yes . . . even food. I can still picture the very wide and long aisles, which reminded me of a bowling alley. After the novelty of the store wore off, my parents stopped shopping there. They complained that the store was just too big and carried too many other things besides groceries.

Every few years since, I've noticed and visited similar store concepts cropping up. One of the latest is the new SuperK stores from Kmart. Imagine, a 40,000-square-foot supermarket inside a Kmart!

France's Carrefour came to Philadelphia and Texas in the early eighties and built megastores of 200,000 square feet. They had to put their customer service reps on roller skates, the stores were so big. They never reached their projected (and needed) sales volume, so they packed up and went home.

As we scan today's retail environment, is the time finally right for the super-sized supermarkets? After all, very large stores like Home Depot, Staples, Office Depot, and Sports Connection are doing very well. Is the supermarket as we know it a dinosaur? Hardly. The reasons for these other superstores' successes have to do a lot with service and value. They focus all their efforts in one area and have become the experts—just as supermarkets are the experts in foodstuffs.

Every retailer is jealous of the supermarket. After all, what other stores do we visit as often, and where else do we spend so much? So other retailers try putting a supermarket inside their store to get us in there more often. But what about us? Do we want to shop there for our foods? As supermarkets strive to keep up with the consumer of the nineties, there's the potentially dangerous possibility of falling into the trap of "merchandising by store size," rather than by paying attention to the consumer. Sure, we are more time constrained than ever before, but does that mean that our number-one motivation is that we want everything we buy under one roof?

If there is any trend in store size that supermarkets should be watching, it's the evolution of the smaller store that specializes in one particular category. To find the new competitors to today's supermarket, watch Beverage Depot, Pet Supply, and even Smokers' Paradise. Smaller stores offer high-quality service and good value—in some cases, even a better understanding of consumer needs. At Pet Supply, for example, pets are welcome to shop with their owners.

But when should we shop where? To get comparative information, we interviewed some of the leading new "category specific" retailers. What we found in almost all cases is that these stores offered a wider selection and more highly trained sales staff. But when it came to pricing, there was little difference relative to the supermarket. In fact, the average supermarket price was sometimes cheaper. See the table on the next page for a variety of examples.

So what's the future of retail? Are we going back to the local neighborhood specialty store (that now is ten times larger than in our grandparents' day), or will these stores and the supermarket fight it out for our dollars?

Product Pricing Comparison

Product	Price at Specialty Store/ Category Buster	Price at Supermarket
Category Store: Auntie Pasta		
Dry pasta (1 lb.)	$1.89	$1.09–$1.45
Pasta sauces	$4.95–$5.95 for 15 oz.	$1.43–$1.79 for 14 oz.
Category Store: Beverages & More		
Pepsi (2-liter bottle)	$1.39	$.79–$1.39
Coca-Cola (six-pack)	$2.39	$2.12–$2.59
O'Doul's nonalcoholic beer (six-pack)	$3.48	$3.69–$4.35
Sharps (six-pack)	$3.48	$3.29–$3.89
Jose Cuervo tequila (750 ml bottle)	$10.98	$12.35–$15.99
Smirnoff vodka (750 ml bottle)	$10.95	$11.55–$14.99
Category Store: PETsMART		
Animal collars (each)	$3.00–$20.00	$3.99–$6.99
Kitty litter	$3.00–$15.00 for 35 lb.	$2.09–$3.99 for 10 lb. $6.99–$8.49 for 14 lb.
Category Store: Home Express		
Brooms and mops (each)	$5.99–$12.99	$4.99–$11.69

Undoubtedly, retailers like Beverages & More and PETsMART are waking up the supermarket retailer. Most of the store personnel I interviewed believed the reasons people shopped at their stores centered around low price, selection, and service (expertise). When looking at prices only, however, it is clear that specialty or category buster stores have similar, if not higher, prices for their products compared to supermarkets. (However, this was a very small scale interview, so use caution in drawing conclusions about nationwide pricing trends. Still, our experiment does shed a little light.)

In terms of selection, one need only visit some of these establishments to see that they have the traditional grocery stores beat. To gather pricing data, we visited each store personally and found that when these stores claim they specialize in certain products, they really do. For example, at Beverages & More, a consumer can purchase traditional soda (such as Coca-Cola or Pepsi) as well as egg cream soda, ginger beer, soda by the keg, hand-brewed soda, and soda with unique flavors. Typically, we cannot find this type of variety in our neighborhood supermarkets. But when it comes to special services (things like delivery, mail orders, and sampling), supermarkets are a viable competitor.

Our conclusion? If you want a wider variety of product than you can find at your supermarket, shop at the category busters. If you are looking for the best value—that combination of quality, service, and price—*and* want one-stop shopping, your supermarket is still the best place to go.

Five Fast Shopping Hints for Working People

In today's stressed-out business world, lots of couples and singles are trying to schedule every minute to the max. Often, a quick bite on the way home from (or on the way to) the office suffices for a meal. And a common complaint is "I just don't have the time to shop."

I too am one of those people who never seem to have enough time (*except* for supermarket shopping, that is). Here are my personally developed and proven-to-work hints that I guarantee will give you enough time to not only go to the supermarket—but make the most of the experience.

Hint #1: Shop Daily

Shop every day if you can. While the idea of saving time by shopping more may at first seem paradoxical, you'll soon see the advantages of a habit that the Europeans have used for centuries. Each day they focus on just the immediate day's meals. True, they have other reasons for shopping daily—less storage and access to lots more fresh foods—but their shopping trips require only a few minutes, as yours will.

Try this tomorrow. Take just a few minutes while you are driving home and think about dinner for that night and breakfast for the next morning. Stop at a supermarket that's on your way home and go in. Don't shop the entire store—cherry pick! Just go directly to the items you need. Never buy more than ten items; the express lane was created just for you. Think of the express lane as a privilege for busy people who shop often.

Hint #2: Shop During Moderately Busy Times

Kelly, the customer service manager at the Albertson's in Portland, Oregon, suggests that the biggest time saver is choosing when to do your shopping. "Make sure you are not hitting the peak times. But do go when the market is moderately busy. During regular hours, the [amount of] staff that they have depends on the amount of traffic. During off hours they might have only one checker, and you'll wait longer."

Hint #3: Find the Fast Lane

Go to the fastest checkout lane. Most times stores have multiple express lanes open, and they are usually your best route out of the store. However, some express checkouts require payment in cash. So what's the fastest checkout lane?

A clerk at a Southern California market suggests looking to see whether or not the checker has a bagger helping. If the checker is doing his or her own bagging, the line will move slower. Also, don't automatically go to the first or last checkstand. Many people end their shopping trip in the last aisle and go immediately to the closest line. This one tends to back up.

Try to make eye contact with the cashier. Does that person look quick? Is he or she alert and with it? Focused on the job or talking to a coworker or to customers?

Hint #4: Shop Only When You Are Ready

Depressed? Had a bad day? Hungry? Cranky? Is this the time to go supermarket shopping? Well, there are conflicting views. The first says never go near a store; you'll spend too much or get more stressed out. The other suggests that supermarket shopping can be great therapy. Being surrounded by all those fresh and colorful foods that smell so good can just about turn around anyone's day.

Psychologist Jackie Persons, Ph.D., is director of the Center for Cognitive Therapy in Oakland, California. She says, "I've done some work in the area of depression and in the area of mood states. My colleagues and I have shown that when you're in a depressed mood state, you're more likely to have certain types of negative thoughts that, when you're not in a depressed mood state, are probably still there; you're just not accessing and reporting them. So when you're in a hungry state, you'll probably be more vulnerable to certain urges and certain thoughts that you don't have when you're in a not-hungry state."

Doris Treatman, a licensed clinical social worker with the Adolescent-Adult Counseling Center in Berkeley, California, comments, "If you're hungry and rushed, you buy fast food that you don't have to go home and cook. When I'm hungry, I buy more on impulse. . . . It's much more impulse buying than it is thoughtful buying. In a checkout line when you're in a hurry, every minute you wait is stressful."

Hint #5: Fax Your Order

More and more supermarkets are accepting fax orders. Just write up your list, fax it in, and your order will be ready for you to pick up at the time you designate—or the store will deliver it to your office or home. Usually you pay for your groceries when you receive them.

Winn-Dixie Stores was one of the first supermarket chains to offer "fax ordering." Mickey Clerc, director of public relations, tells how it works: "If you live in a home-delivery area, there will be catalogs at your Winn-Dixie store that include a fax order form. Or you can fax our 800 number, and they will fax your local Winn-Dixie number and location." The toll-free numbers for Winn-Dixie are (800) 333-5478 (fax) and (800) 284-7467 (phone).

To make the process easier, get the catalog with the fax order form at your local store. That way you can use the catalog numbers to identify products. When you place an order, include your home address, work and home phone numbers, the date you're ordering, and the date you'd like delivery. On the order form, select one of the listed delivery times based on the time you will be home to receive the order. Remember to indicate A.M. or P.M. Indicate whether you'll accept substitutions and whether you'll be using manufacturer coupons. Record how you'll be paying—by check or credit card. If paying with a credit card, specify the kind of card (Visa, MasterCard, Discover, etc.), your account number, and the expiration date. Remember to list the quantity of each item you're ordering along with the catalog number.

Store charges vary by chain. Even if your store does not have a formal fax ordering service, it's well worth asking the manager if you can order by fax anyway.

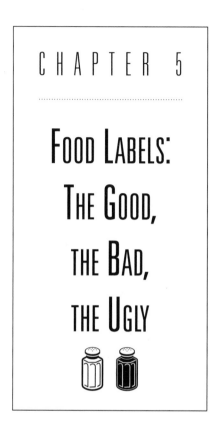

CHAPTER 5

FOOD LABELS: THE GOOD, THE BAD, THE UGLY

Are you confused about the differences among low fat, reduced fat, and no fat? Well, you are not alone. As Americans are striving to find the best (and most healthful) foods, we are finding that search to be sometimes difficult and confusing.

Prevention magazine and the Food Marketing Institute, in their Shopping for Health 1995 nationwide survey, report that 34 percent of shoppers surveyed stopped buying a particular product because of what they read on the label. With this kind of influence, it's easy to see why manufacturers are trying hard to create packages that "sell" us on the health attributes of their products. According to the Shopping for Health survey, many of us are confused and frustrated. Forty-four percent of the respondents either strongly or mostly agreed there is so much conflicting information about foods that they don't know what to eat anymore. Three-quarters (76 percent) think too many foods claim to be "healthy."

And this survey was conducted just a bit more than a year after the "new and improved" nutritional labels hit the shelves. There's lots of discussion about what's right and wrong with the new labels. According to the Food and Drug Administration (FDA), "The purpose of the food label reform was simple: to clear up confusion that has prevailed on supermarket shelves for years, to help consumers choose more healthful diets, and to offer an incentive to food companies to improve the nutritional qualities of their products."

WHY THE FDA SAYS THE NUTRITIONAL LABEL WILL HELP CONSUMERS

Virginia Wilkening, R.D., of the FDA's Office of Food Labeling, explains the benefits of the new food labels.

First, she points out, the regulations make nutrition labeling mandatory for almost all processed foods. Furthermore, the labels must include information that once was voluntary or even prohibited. For example, the labels must now include information on the amounts of saturated fat and cholesterol—formerly voluntary. The nutritional listing of fiber and sugars weren't permitted under the old regulations. With the new label, consumers have information about these and other nutrients, which can help them choose their food more wisely.

Something else is new on our labels—a column labeled "% Daily Value." According to Wilkening, this information is designed to simplify label reading (and hopefully nutrition planning). The declaration of this percentage allows the consumer to figure the nutrient content of a food into the context of a total daily diet. That way, there is less calculating for those trying to keep track of their daily allowances of certain nutrients, and people can better compare the percentage with that of a similar serving size for a similar product.

Another advantage identified by Wilkening is special requirements for food targeted to young children. The labels on foods for children under two, excluding baby formula, may not provide information about certain fat-related nutrients and cholesterol. The reason for this is to discourage parents from limiting their babies' fat intake, as fat is important for health in those early years. Similarly, the labels on food for children under four may not carry % Daily Values for certain nutrients because the FDA hasn't established Daily Values for these nutrients for this particular age group.

Serving sizes under the current law are more uniform, not simply subject to the manufacturer's discretion. A serving size on a nutrition label must represent amounts of a food people have actually been found to eat. This amount must be stated using standard measurements called for in the law. Before serving sizes were standardized, consumers often had difficulty comparing the nutritional information of similar foods.

Nutritional information is now easy to locate, says Wilkening. This is because the regulations specify the location and type sizes of the panels for the "Nutrition Facts" information. The nutritional information must appear on the first panel to the right of the principal display panel. The exact specifications for the size and kind of type to be used on this panel and in all labeling on the package have made the label easier to read.

WHY OTHERS THINK THE NEW LABELS AREN'T ENOUGH

Since these regulations were first issued, there has been lots of publicity about the ways consumers are being misled. Some complaints have been justified, as companies have either ignored the regulations or figured out ways around them. The on-pack promises of good taste or health are powerful motivations to a marketer. The FDA is monitoring these, but most times, consumer complaints are what alerts the FDA to misleading claims. The Center for Science in the Public Interest (CSPI), a Washington, D.C.–based advocacy group, has done more than anyone to alert consumers to products that are deceptive.

While CSPI and others are making sure the word gets out on these products (and in some cases working with manufacturers to correct the problem areas), don't just rely on their activities. Always read the ingredients list and Nutrition Facts to determine whether the product lives up to the claims or description on the package.

In CSPI's *Nutrition Action Health Letter* (May 1995), Bonnie Leibman offers these examples of deceptive ingredient claims that have evaded the new regulations:

- Pillsbury pumpkin bread—"Made with real Pumpkin!" crows the label. But CSPI estimates that each one-ounce serving contains only about one teaspoon of dried pumpkin.
- Multi-Grain Cheerios—The box says they're made ". . . with a Touch of Brown Sugar." But in addition to the "touch" of brown sugar, this cereal also contains about five grams per serving of regular (white) sugar.
- Campbell's Healthy Request chicken with rice soup—A serving of this soup contains a measly ½ teaspoon of chicken and 3½ teaspoons of rice—and the label doesn't need to say how much.
- Kellogg's Nutri-Grain waffles—The label claims these are "Made with Whole Grain Wheat," but

there's more refined flour than whole-wheat flour. In fact, there's more water than whole-wheat flour.

■ Smucker's Simply Fruit—The label calls it "Spreadable Fruit," but the small print indicates it is "100% Fruit Sweetened with Concentrated Fruit Juices." In fact, there's more white grape juice than fruit.

■ Frookie chocolate-chip cookies—"Fruit Juice Added," reads the label, but it's just vitamin-less grape and apple juice. Check the ingredients list, and you'll also find organic evaporated sugar cane juice—"no better than ordinary sugar," says CSPI.

David Schardt, associate nutritionist at CSPI, shares his thoughts on what he views as another deficiency in the new labels—the absence of listings for certain vitamin nutrients. He cautions that different subgroups of people have different vitamin deficiencies and, sometimes needs for vitamins are even more individual than that. "However, vitamins that do come up are folic acid, the intake of which inhibits birth defects, Vitamin B_6, and Vitamin B_{12} for older people."

We asked Schardt how consumers can find out how much of these unspecified nutrients are in the food. "Many will have weights measured in micrograms and milligrams, which are very small amounts to try to verify on your own," said Schardt. "Consulting reference books that have nutritional contents of foods may help; certain references might also help consumers identify the best sources of nutrients and vitamins they need for special diets."

CSPI is focusing its efforts on identifying and exposing misleading *ingredient* claims. These are the implied marketing claims that manufacturers believe will add consumer draw to their products. David Schardt offers examples: "Aunt Jemima's blueberry waffles is mostly a mouthful of Crisco and does not contain any fruit." He lists the most common ingredient claim terms that CSPI feels can be misleading:

- "Natural"
- "With *real* fruit"
- "Veggies"
- "Whole grains"
- "Lightly sweetened"

In addition to CSPI's list, here are some other commonly misleading words found on front labels:

- Made from concentrate
- Organic
- No sugar added
- No fat
- Vitamin added
- Vitamin enriched

A good rule of thumb: When you see these claims (or any other health claims, for that matter) on the front of the package, turn the package around and look carefully at both the ingredients list and the Nutrition Facts label to make sure you know what you are getting. Spending a few minutes more at the point of purchase guarantees that you won't bring home a product that you'll be dissatisfied with—or one that has wasted your money!

THE WORDS AND WHAT THEY ARE SUPPOSED TO MEAN

"What does *fresh* mean?" This question is asked more than any other. The FDA's definition states that *fresh* can be used only on a food that is raw, has never been frozen or heated, and contains no preservatives—but irradiation at low levels is allowed. It's a very confusing definition. Simply put, fresh is supposed to imply a product that has not ever been modified through temperature or by using a preservative to extend its shelf life. The irradiation process needs much clarification, and we'll discuss it later in this chapter.

Many consumers have been fooled by seemingly fresh products that have been previously frozen and later thawed. While the FDA's regulations do prohibit this practice, it is very difficult to monitor and to catch. Beware of meats, poultry, seafood, and other fresh foods that are harder in the middle than at the edges. Make sure the package (especially if it's a plastic wrap) fits the product properly. Thawing and refreezing will usually create a misfitting package. Look for extra juices that might be caused by condensation from thawing.

If you suspect that a product marked and sold as "fresh" has any of these signs, ask the department or store manager directly if this product was delivered to the store fresh or frozen. Many refrigerated trucks and warehouses are kept slightly above freezing to ensure proper handling. If the product has been in too cold an environment, it will partially or completely freeze—which can affect the product's taste, texture, or nutritive value.

How Reading Secret Manufacturer Codes Can Help You Choose Fresher Products

What is freshness anyway? It's harder to tell than ever with the variety of freshness codes, open dating, sell-by dates, and packed-by dates appearing on different products. Unfortunately, as of yet, there is no standard regulation governing all products sold in the supermarket to ease our confusion. So until that happens, we must take the time to understand exactly what we are reading.

Freshness Dating

The good news is that the freshness dating must be clearly understood and readable. For example, "sell by [date]," means exactly that. The product should be sold by this date. (Conversely, we shouldn't buy the product after this date.) After that date, the product is not necessarily spoiled—just past its prime usage span. How much time after this date you should consume the product depends on the type of product and packaging. My best advice is to call the consumer hotline 800 number on the package before you consume.

In the Grocery Manufacturers Association's nationwide Consumer Trend Study of 1,005 shoppers in 1995, the number-one trend "on the way up" was paying attention to freshness dating (rating slightly higher than buying reduced-fat foods). And it appears that manufacturers are listening, as more and more products contain open (meaning readable to us consumers) dating.

The ability of consumers to actually read the freshness coding on most food packages is a relatively recent phenomenon. Sure, milk and lots of other dairy products have had the open dating for a while—but for most of the products in the supermarket, it's an innovation.

Milk has led the way in establishing the perceived importance of freshness. The surprise-hit movie *Clerks* chronicles the adventures of a convenience store employee. One scene (which was particularly enjoyed by the audience in the theater where I watched the movie) focuses on the freshness dating of milk and how consumers search among all the packages, destroying the shelves to find that one carton with the longest code date. The camera follows a woman shopper who takes every milk carton off the shelf, placing them around her on the floor till she can reach the one in the back. Finally satisfied that she has found the ultimate date code, she leaves the store with the remaining cartons still on the floor. In the movie, we learn that this type of shopper has been nicknamed one of the "milk maids" and is the only customer to really get under the clerk's skin.

I happen to be one of those consumers who search way in the back for the milk marked with the longest code. And with two good reasons: First, I want to get the freshest milk possible. And second, I know that the milk in the back of the case is the coldest! But I never leave the shelves a mess!

Rob Byrne, Ph.D., director of product safety and technology for the International Dairy Foods Association, gives us the facts about the dating of milk: All states require sell-by dates, but there is no consistent requirement of how many days before the product spoils. The factor that most affects shelf life is temperature. The recommended temperature, in the store and at home, is 40 to 45 degrees Fahrenheit. Dairies typically "short-date" the milk by seven to ten days to ensure that they meet the regulations and we drink the milk at its peak. That means the actual "drink by" date can be about a week later than the date stamped on the container.

What about other products? Recently Pepsi started what I suspect will be a major trend: the advertising and branding of freshness. Gary Hemphill of Pepsi's consumer relations explains, "Freshness dating is another tool for the shopper to consume the product at peak freshness." Freshness? of a Pepsi? Yes! In fact, according to Pepsi, when stored correctly (refrigerated or at room temperature), Diet Pepsi will stay at peak flavor for only about 100 days. This is because Nutrasweet loses flavor over time. If you store the product in a warm area, it will lose sweetness faster. So much for the misconception that if it's in a can, it will last forever. This applies not only to Diet Pepsi, but to all beverages and other products that contain Nutrasweet.

Temperature Control

One of the most critical ways to maintain freshness in any product is to maintain the optimal temperature. We can do our part and control storage at home, but what about before the product gets to us? Manufacturers and retailers must ensure that product temperatures in shipping and storage are at the proper levels. If you see ice cream that's soft in the freezer case, or milk that's not cold, you don't buy it. You know it won't last as long. The same rule (perhaps not in the same extreme) pertains to all fresh products.

Other Codes on Packages

But what about those codes and numbers on the package that we can't read? What are those? Can they help us choose a product? They certainly can. In fact, they may be one of the most valuable tools in deciphering the freshness (or staleness) of a product.

Manufacturer codes have long been one of the great mysteries of the supermarket. Most of us have stared at those jumbled letters and numbers, wondering what they meant. Some of us even wonder why there's a need for a secret code. Unfortunately, just as in the case of freshness dating, there is no mandatory or universal standard.

The easiest way to decipher these is to call a manufacturer's toll-free customer service line and ask. But that's not always possible, especially while you're shopping. Here are some basic guidelines that you can follow to help figure out the codes yourself. Keep in mind that each manufacturer might follow a different procedure, so you may want to call and get the individual code of any company whose products you buy often.

1. Manufacturer codes are typically located near the expiration date or at the top of the package. Most codes are imprinted at time of product manufacture, so look for an embossed or ink-jet series of letters and numbers. As an example, we will use a box of General Mills' Bugles. On the top of the box is the code J528W3.

2. The first letter, *J*, denotes the month the Bugles were manufactured. Don't be confused—*J* does not mean January or June. Most food companies start their manufacturing year in June and start their coding with the letter *A*. June = A, July = B, and so on. The exception is the letter *I*, which is never used, to avoid the possible confusion with the number 1. So, counting down the months, we find that *J* refers to February.

3. The first number, 5, refers to the last number in the year of manufacture. Since few foods have a ten-year shelf life, it is safe to assume that it refers to 1995.

4. The next two numbers, 2 and 8, are the exact day of manufacture: 28. So far, with J528, we have deciphered the manufacturing date: February 28, 1995. Remember that this date is the date the product was made and does not refer to the freshness or expiration date. Some products are manufactured two months or more before they are delivered to the supermarket.

5. Next we have the *W*. Here's where you have to call the manufacturer to get clarification. Most times, it is a plant designation and tells us the city of manufacture. In this instance, by calling General Mills I learned that *W* is the code for the company's West Chicago plant.

6. Last, we see a 3. Here again, checking with the manufacturer is important, and we discover that it means
"third shift." Depending on the manufacturer, it could
mean a particular shift, crew, or machine.

So what we've uncovered is that this box of Bugles was
made on February 28, 1995, in the company's West
Chicago plant on the third shift. Why is that important?
If you have a complaint about product quality, knowing
how to read these codes can help the company track down
the problem. And in the case of a product recall, you can
immediately tell if you have a particular package of the
recalled product—even if the information on television or
in the newspaper is incomplete.

Most importantly, you can tell how fresh a product is by
yourself. You can calculate the time between manufacture
and the time you find it on the shelf and compare it to the
freshness or sell-by date that may be on the package. Now
you can really choose the best-tasting and freshest foods.

FREQUENTLY MISUNDERSTOOD WORDS: TEACH YOURSELF TO TRANSLATE

Another one of the most confusing labeling laws surrounds
the word *free*. The implication is that when coupled with

fat, sugar, calories, or *sodium, free* means "lack of." You would think so, but it's not true. According to the FDA, fat- or sugar-free means less than 0.5 grams per serving; sodium-free and calorie-free mean less than 5 grams.

So does our basic understanding of words change when we walk into the supermarket? Unfortunately yes, and hence both the confusion and the need for this primer. Especially as we see more new healthy foods on the shelves each day. (*Healthy,* by the way, can only be used on a label if the food is low in fat and in saturated fat and a serving contains no more than 480 milligrams of sodium and 60 milligrams of cholesterol. But buyer beware, that definition only applies to *healthy* as a claim— not when used as part of the brand name, as in Healthy Choice, Healthy Request, or Good Health.)

This chapter includes the basic regulations and definitions in an easy-to-read reference. If you want a much more complete guide to the Nutrition Facts label, you can request a copy directly from the FDA. I've found that one of the easiest-to-read and most complete of their publications is entitled "A Food Labeling Guide," published in September 1994. Each guideline is well illustrated and explained in a question-and-answer format. Every answer is cross-referenced with the actual FDA regulation identification number, which makes it easy to trace for further explanation if you so desire. You can order a copy (there may be a nominal charge) from your local FDA district office or from the U.S. Government Printing Office, Washington, D.C. 20402, telephone (202) 783-3238.

Remember that all of the regulations in the following examples (and on all food packages) are based on the serving size listed at the top of the package's nutrition label. Start there, and if you think you'll eat more than, for example, one ounce of potato chips (approximately six chips), multiply the realistic serving size for you by the nutritional data.

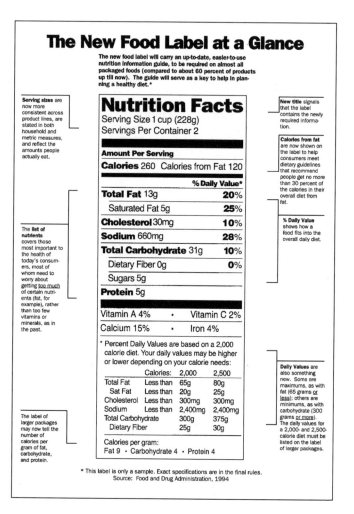

The New Food Label at a Glance

The new food label will carry an up-to-date, easier-to-use nutrition information guide, to be required on almost all packaged foods (compared to about 60 percent of products up till now). The guide will serve as a key to help in planning a healthy diet.*

Serving sizes are now more consistent across product lines, are stated in both household and metric measures, and reflect the amounts people actually eat.

New title signals that the label contains the newly required information.

Calories from fat are now shown on the label to help consumers meet dietary guidelines that recommend people get no more than 30 percent of the calories in their overall diet from fat.

Nutrition Facts

Serving Size 1 cup (228g)
Servings Per Container 2

Amount Per Serving

Calories 260   Calories from Fat 120

	% Daily Value*
Total Fat 13g	**20**%
Saturated Fat 5g	**25**%
Cholesterol 30mg	**10**%
Sodium 660mg	**28**%
Total Carbohydrate 31g	**10**%
Dietary Fiber 0g	**0**%
Sugars 5g	
Protein 5g	

Vitamin A 4%	•	Vitamin C 2%
Calcium 15%	•	Iron 4%

The **list of nutrients** covers those most important to the health of today's consumers, most of whom need to worry about getting too much of certain nutrients (fat, for example), rather than too few vitamins or minerals, as in the past.

% Daily Value shows how a food fits into the overall daily diet.

* Percent Daily Values are based on a 2,000 calorie diet. Your daily values may be higher or lower depending on your calorie needs:

	Calories:	2,000	2,500
Total Fat	Less than	65g	80g
Sat Fat	Less than	20g	25g
Cholesterol	Less than	300mg	300mg
Sodium	Less than	2,400mg	2,400mg
Total Carbohydrate		300g	375g
Dietary Fiber		25g	30g

Calories per gram:
Fat 9 • Carbohydrate 4 • Protein 4

Daily Values are also something new. Some are maximums, as with fat (65 grams or less); others are minimums, as with carbohydrate (300 grams or more). The daily values for a 2,000- and 2,500-calorie diet must be listed on the label of larger packages.

The label of larger packages may now tell the number of calories per gram of fat, carbohydrate, and protein.

* This label is only a sample. Exact specifications are in the final rules.
Source: Food and Drug Administration, 1994

The New Food Label at a Glance

Claims: While descriptive terms like "low," "good source," and "free" have long been used on food labels, their meaning — and their usefulness in helping consumers plan a healthy diet — have been murky. Now FDA has set specific definitions for these terms, assuring shoppers that they can believe what they read on the package.

Ingredients still will be listed in descending order by weight, and now the list will be required on almost all foods, even standardized ones like mayonnaise and bread.

FROZEN MIXED VEGETABLES
IN SAUCE

NET WT. 8.9 oz. (252 g)

Ingredients: Broccoli, carrots, green beans, water chestnuts, soybean oil, milk solids, modified cornstarch, salt, spices.

"While many factors affect heart disease, diets low in saturated fat and cholesterol may reduce the risk of this disease."

Source: Food and Drug Administration, 1994

Health Claims: For the first time, food labels will be allowed to carry information about the link between certain nutrients and specific diseases. For such a "health claim" to be made on a package, FDA must first determine that the diet-disease link is supported by scientific evidence.

Health claim message referred to on the front panel is shown here.

Let's start by taking a look at some of the most misunderstood and confusing terms that are used in packaging: claims about fat, cholesterol, sugar, and "light" foods.

Claims About Fat

"Fat," according to a *Prevention* magazine/FMI study, "is the primary reason for putting foods in or taking them out of the grocery basket." See if these FDA definitions match what you think:

Fat free..................less than 0.5 g fat per serving

Low fat ....3 g or less per serving

Low saturated fat....1 g or less per serving and not more than 15 percent of calories from saturated fatty acids

Reduced (or less)
fat......................At least 25 percent less fat per serving than the food that it is being compared to

Claims About Cholesterol

"Cholesterol free" and "fat free" are sometimes confused.

Cholesterol free ......Less than 2 mg cholesterol and 2 g or less saturated fat per serving

Low cholesterol ......20 mg or less cholesterol and 2 g or less saturated fat

Reduced (or less)
cholesterol..........At least 25 percent less cholesterol per serving than the food it is being compared to and 2 g or less saturated fat

Claims About Sugar and Calories

With the introduction of more fat-free foods, we are seeing sugar being used as a fat replacement. Check out the ingredients list. (Remember that ingredients are always listed in descending order based on content by weight.) You may be surprised to learn that a fat-free product is very high in calories and sugar.

"No added sugar" or "no sugar added" do in fact mean the same thing: no sugars were *added* in processing or packing. But it doesn't mean sugar free.

Sugar free ....Less than 0.5 g sugar per serving

Low calorie.............40 calories or less per serving

Reduced calorie ......At least 25 percent fewer calories per serving than the food referred to

"Lite" and "Light" Foods

Understandably, one of the most misunderstood terms is *Light*, often spelled *Lite:*

Light or Lite...........Can mean ⅓ fewer calories or ½ the fat of the referenced food; or the sodium content of an already low-fat, low-calorie food has been reduced by 50 percent; or the food is lighter in color or texture (as long as there is information on the label qualifying what *light* means)

My suggestion is that when you see the word *light* on a label, make sure you understand its use. I see more flagrant misuse of this term than of any other.

Remember, most claims fall into these categories: free, low, reduced, or light. The nutritional labels are there to help us—and they do. But we can't blindly rely on on-pack claims. We have a responsibility to read that ingredients list and have a basic understanding of these terms.

Other Claims

Some additional words starting to appear on the front of our food packages aren't *as* confusing, but they still need a bit of clarification:

Lean can be used to describe the fat content of meat, poultry, seafood, and game.

Lean......................Less than 10 g fat and 4.5 g or less saturated fat and less than 95 mg cholesterol per serving (100 g)

Extra lean...............Less than 5 g fat and less than 2 g saturated fat and less than 95 mg cholesterol per serving (100 g)

High can be used if a food contains 20 percent or more of the Daily Value for a particular nutrient. An example is breakfast cereal that proclaims, "High in vitamin C." This cereal must have at least 60 milligrams of vitamin C—20 percent of the Reference Daily Intake (RDI) for vitamin C set by the National Academy of Sciences.

Good source means that one serving contains 10 to 19 percent of the Daily Value for a nutrient.

More means a serving of an unaltered or altered food contains at least 10 percent more of the Daily Value of a nutrient than the referenced food. This term is used in comparisons on packages and in advertising.

Top 10 Misleading Labeling Claims

One of the most frustrating experiences in putting together this discussion of labeling was trying to determine which of the misleading claims are most common. While the FDA and Freedom of Information Act staff were helpful, such data apparently have not yet been compiled. FDA staff did, however, offer these ten claims that they feel are the most misleading to consumers:

1. "High energy" or "high calorie"
2. "Low sugar"
3. "Good source" or "high" claims for a nutrient without a Daily Value (for example, "high in omega-3 fatty acids")
4. "Sugar free"
5. "Low"
6. Cholesterol claims
7. "___ % fat free" on products that are not low fat
8. "Fat free"
9. "No sugar added"
10. "Free" or "low" claims for foods that are always free or low in the nutrient (for example, "fat-free broccoli" in place of "broccoli, a fat-free food")

These claims break down into two main categories. The first three are what FDA staff call "claims that have not been defined and therefore may not be used." If you see these words on the package, you should be immediately suspicious and check both the Nutrition Facts label and the ingredients list. The second category is "claims being used when the food (itself) does not qualify." The only way to test these claims is to check the nutritional data and ingredients. If you have any questions about the legitimacy of these claims, call the manufacturer directly or contact the FDA office nearest your home.

When Is "Healthy" Not?

Lots of products and advertising are using the word *healthy* to describe themselves. But as with the claims just discussed, sometimes a product uses the term *healthy* to imply that the product has more nutritional benefits than it actually does. Some of the best discussion and examples on the subject are in an article entitled "Healthy Foods Due for a Checkup" (*Tufts University Diet and Nutrition Letter*, July 1994):

> ConAgra's Healthy Choice Butter Pecan Crunch meets healthy requirements: no more than 3 grams fat, 1 g sat fat, 480 mg of sodium or 60 mg cholesterol. Also meets the DV for one major nutrient—calcium.
>
> Campbell's Healthy Request beef vegetable soup, over 480 mg sodium. So do Healthy Choice

Garden Potato Casserole, Budget Gourmet's Light, Healthy Herbed Chicken Breast with Fettuccini, and Healthy Choice's baked cooked ham slices.

Wish-Bone Healthy Sensation 1000 Island dressing is OK for sodium but lacks 10% of any key nutrients. The government's response: reformulate the products to meet the new guidelines by the end of next year or get the word 'healthy' out of the name. The same goes for products that don't have 'healthy' in the title but make the 'healthy' claim somewhere else on the label. (Note: according to Janet McDonald, FDA, those regulations didn't come into effect till 1/96, though new products coming out now are required to comply immediately.)

Main-dish requirements differ—3 g of fat for every 3.5 ounces, no more than 600 mg sodium by '95, but 480 mg by end '97.

Meat, poultry, fish can be 'healthy' with up to 5 g of fat per serving, 2 g of sat fat and 95 mg cholesterol.

Each case and example leads directly to the same conclusion: We have a responsibility to check nutritional facts and ingredients on the package. The FDA has just too much monitoring and inspection to do with the current staffing and regulations. Don't assume that just because a product is on the shelf, the government has approved the label or that it's correct "because someone else is checking."

WHAT ABOUT
ORGANIC PRODUCTS?

It used to be that if you wanted to buy organically grown foods, you had to go to a health food store—and even there your selection could be somewhat limited. Then the nationwide panic over Alar hit the headlines, and practically every supermarket in America started carrying organic (pesticide-free) produce.

Loosely defined, *organically grown* refers to a product that is pesticide and chemical free both in growing and in processing. The primary benefit for most consumers is a better-tasting and more nutritious product. A valuable side benefit is more earth-friendly food production.

But consumers soon realized that organic food looked different. The apples weren't quite as red and shiny, and they had blemishes. Prices were in some cases double what we were used to paying. These reasons were enough for most shoppers not to even try organic produce. Supermarkets that didn't understand how to merchandise or handle it quickly began discontinuing it.

While some shoppers had their taste buds awakened, they also began an entirely new approach to label reading. Most had to go to health food stores to even find and experiment with organically grown foods. And the question of what's really "organic" surfaced.

Since then the FDA and U.S. Department of Agriculture (USDA) have been trying to establish a national standard for growers to follow. They're getting closer, but until then we have to rely on the individual states' certifications, which do vary.

Don't trust the words *organically grown* on the front of the label unless it states clearly the type of certification to which the product adheres. Certification standards are currently determined by state regulations governing the length of time the soil has been kept free from pesticides or other chemicals, as well as contamination from nonorganic fields and products.

Will organics become a commonplace reality? Linda Gilbert, president of Health Focus, a Des Moines–based marketing research firm specializing in the healthy foods market, conducts an annual healthy foods survey. Gilbert believes, "The growth of organics will be a lot slower than a lot of other people in the organics world would like to think." She breaks down the growth potential into three consumer benefits: (1) purity, especially applicable to health and beauty aids, baby foods, and pet foods; (2) quality, which we find featured mostly in gourmet foods like coffee, juices, and jams; and (3) wholesomeness, associated with salads, breads, and pancake mixes.

According to Nell Newman (daughter of Paul), who heads up the organic division of Newman's Own, the timing is now. Her formula for their organic products' success is based on lots of common sense and a keen understanding of the way people eat. When she first broached the idea to her dad, she started by picking a product that she knew he'd love: "Dad's favorite snack is popcorn (late-night snack) and second is pretzels (late afternoon)." Nell convinced her dad to expand their product line into organics with a simple strategy: "Wouldn't it be great to make great-tasting products that happen to be organic?!"

Newman's first organic products were the "dad-tested" pretzels, made with unbleached wheat and rye flour, brown rice sweetener, barley malt, and sunflower oil. They are certified organic in accordance with California's Organic Foods Act of 1990, which currently has the strictest regulations. Newman has also introduced organic chocolate bars and has plans to add more products.

One of the reasons organics might just become commonplace in the supermarket is the variety of new organic introductions and understanding of consumer trends. Ayla's Organics has introduced a line of eight organic salad dressings, all oil free and very flavor intense. Vermont Gold has introduced a 100 percent pure maple syrup in an Italian-style bottle with an award-winning contemporary label design. Garden of Eatin's product line includes tortilla chips, salsa red chips, and Bible Bagels.

Organic foods, according to Information Resources Inc. of Chicago, are one of the few areas of the supermarket with double-digit growth. Right now organic products are more expensive than their nonorganic counterparts, so some consumers are reluctant to switch. As more companies like Newman's Own introduce organic foods, the selection will increase and, according to Nell Newman, "The prices will come down."

Supermarkets are starting to carry more and more organics. In some stores you have to search for the products in the gourmet or specialty section, but most are integrating the products alongside their nonorganic counterparts. Want to try organics? I'd suggest you follow Paul Newman's lead—start with products you normally eat, rather than an unfamiliar product you have to acquire a taste for.

IRRADIATED PRODUCTS AND HOW THEY ARE LABELED

One of the most controversial labeling issues is irradiation. In this case it's not what to say or how to say it, but whether to say it at all.

Food irradiation is the process of treating foods with gamma radiation from radioactive cobalt, cesium, or other sources, in order to produce x-rays that will extend the shelf life and preservation of foods and/or kill microorganisms and insects.

The benefits of irradiation are limited to certain foods: It can delay spoilage of fresh fish, reduce microorganisms in spices, destroy disease-causing parasites, and extend the shelf life of fruit. In addition, meat, poultry, fish, and some vegetables also can benefit. The good news therefore is that irradiation delays ripening and spoilage and, according to some sources, is a safe and effective way to eliminate harmful bacteria (including salmonella) and parasites.

Two major questions are the focus of this labeling battle. The first is the safety of the radiation itself. The second is the difficulty for a consumer to determine, without some kind of labeling, whether the product has been irradiated.

The FDA has already approved irradiation of certain foods—poultry, pork, and some fruits and vegetables. But they aren't currently being irradiated and sold on the market. The reasons are the real need to educate consumers about the safety of irradiation and the fears expressed by consumer groups about the process and its supposed health risks. In the meantime, the FDA has raised the level of acceptable dosage to three kiloGrays from one, saying that further FDA animal tests have revealed no cancers. It is currently considering petitions for approval to irradiate beef and seafood.

Our issue in this chapter is to help you clearly identify irradiated products and make your own choices. Labeling for irradiated products consists of the internationally known radura symbol and the statement that the food has been "treated by irradiation." *Only* primary products (meats, vegetables, and so on) that have been treated require this labeling, whereas spices or any food that is merely an ingredient do not need to be identified. Based on what the FDA perceives as a need for consumer education from various consumer surveys, the FDA recommends labeling for informational purposes, not as warnings. This symbol can be found on the label near the manufacturer's name and address or as a separate sticker.

Who to Contact with Questions About Food Labeling

FDA Office of Consumer Affairs
HFE-88
Rockville, MD 20856

FDA Seafood Hotline:
(800) 332-4010 (24 hours)

USDA Meat and Poultry Hotline:
(800) 535-4555 (24 hours)
Home economists and dietitians may call
10 A.M.–4 P.M. Monday–Friday.

National Center for Nutrition and Dietetics, American Dietetic Association, Consumer Nutrition Hotline:
(800) 366-1655 (recorded messages
9 A.M.–9 P.M. EDT, Monday–Friday.)
Dietitians may call 10 A.M.–5 P.M. Monday–Friday.

For written information and to have specific labeling questions answered, contact:
FDA/USDA Food Labeling Education
Information Center
National Agricultural Library
10301 Baltimore Blvd., Room 304
Beltsville, MD 20705-2351
(301) 504-5719; fax (301) 505-6409

CHAPTER 6

....

HOW TO CONTACT PRODUCT MANUFACTURERS AND GET SATISFACTION

With over 35,000 products in our supermarkets, it's only natural that from time to time people complain about some of them. A product occasionally may not live up to our expectations, or a defect may slip through the company's procedures for quality control. What makes the difference is how a company responds to our complaints. Are employees responsive? Are they concerned? Do they admit the company's mistake? Do you get the feeling they want to keep you as a customer?

Mary Ellen Gowin, vice president of consumer affairs at Wakefern Food Corporation (the member cooperative for ShopRite Supermarkets in the Northeast), told me some years ago that her department considers consumer complaints as its number-one priority. The reasoning? For every complaint made, more shoppers may have the same problem, and every person who complains and doesn't get a satisfactory response tells an average of sixteen other people.

If you are dissatisfied with a product, first notify the customer service or store manager where you shop. This person can handle most problems, especially if you simply want a product replacement.

At times, the issue is much more complicated, and you will need to contact the manufacturer directly. Many of the products on your supermarket's shelves today list the toll-free number of the manufacturer's consumer affairs department. That number is the place to voice your complaints—and also one of your best resources for recipes, coupons, and rebates.

TEN STEPS FOR COMPLAINING AND GETTING THE FASTEST RESULTS

Here are steps you should follow if and when you have to make a complaint:

1. Start with the courtesy counter in the supermarket where you made the purchase. Keep in mind that the store has employees there to help you resolve your problem. Don't take your frustrations out on them—they didn't create the problem.

2. State the situation and get to the problem quickly.

3. If the courtesy clerk can't help, ask to speak with the department manager, then the store manager. If none of them can help, ask for the telephone number of the corporate buyer.

4. Reaffirm your loyalty to the store and your appreciation of their past efforts in helping to resolve any problems you have experienced. Make sure you don't sound like a chronic complainer.

5. Let the store's personnel know that if you don't get satisfaction from them, you'll keep going all the way to the top.

6. If you are referred to the corporate office, put your complaint in writing and direct it to the president or CEO of the chain. This is particularly effective when the guy in charge has his name on the door.

7. If you are writing a letter, be prepared and to the point—just the facts, copies of packaging or serial number, and a few words to reiterate your loyalty to the store and state your confidence that the company will resolve the situation for you.

8. In person, on the phone, or in a letter, always state what you want—a refund? replacement? compensation for damage?—and when you expect it.

9. Keep copies of all correspondence and notes of any telephone and in-person meetings.

10. Be nice but firm. Make the store's employees want to keep you as a customer.

Guidelines Based on Experience

To see how leading food manufacturers would respond to consumers, we contacted fourteen different food manufacturers (with ten letters and ten phone calls). From the experience comes some guidance—and tips to get the results you deserve. Each of these contacts was directed to the customer service department, not to a particular executive or manager.

Of the ten letters, eight registered complaints about products and two offered praise. Of the phone calls, five registered complaints, and five praise. The complaints generally centered around a problem with the products themselves—for example, stale products, too salty chips and soups (that were supposed to be low salt), faulty packaging, and oily products.

The letters proved the most effective, leading to responses in an average of twenty-one days. Four of these were accompanied by a coupon for a free product. Three of the letters included checks to compensate for our "bad" experience using the product. One included coupons and recipes as compensation.

Seven of the complaint letters specifically asked for some type of reimbursement. All of these requests were granted by the manufacturer. The one letter that did not request reimbursement still yielded a check and product pamphlets. The two letters that praised products also produced high-value coupons.

As stated earlier, it's important to include all the information about the complaint and also to clearly state what you expect. In the rare instances where you or your family's health or well-being is involved, my suggestion is to discuss the situation with an attorney or other professional before you contact the manufacturer.

In writing a complaint letter, try to direct it to the person most empowered to resolve your situation. If you are concerned about a political issue, address it to the CEO or person responsible for government affairs; if it's an advertising issue, send it to the head of marketing or advertising. And if it's a product complaint, address it directly to the product manager or the customer relations manager. Typically, you can get these names and addresses by calling the toll-free number on the package or by looking them up in a library, on-line database, or trade magazine or association directory.

Before you send a message, think it through so you will be clear. Here's one of the sample letters we sent out. Read it and think about how you could make it more effective:

Dear Customer Service Rep:

I am writing to you because I am slightly irritated with the contents of one of your products, New England Clam Chowder. It tasted rather strange, to be honest, and I didn't feel right even finishing it, I'm afraid to say. Why would this be? I tried to think of different reasons, but I've come up empty, and I need some help. I hope the staff there could point me in the right direction on this so that I don't come across the same problem again.

The can has the numbers XY 4356 (19 oz.) on it, if you need that information. Otherwise, I'd say that it seemed to have a taste other than chowder. I know what chowder tastes like because I used to live in New England and my father worked clamming on a boat in the harbor. We used to eat them all the time and in various forms, so I know my clams.

I would appreciate some token of acknowledgment from you on this, just so I know that nothing's wrong in the production process, or something like that.

How would you respond to such a letter if you had to answer it? Put yourself in the place of a person who wants to make you happy and keep you as a loyal customer. What were the key points made? Did the person seem to have a legitimate complaint—or just to want something for free?

In our test, three of the five telephone complaint calls had not been responded to sixty days later. The consumer complaints included damage to personal belongings through product use, bad-tasting water, and products being too salty. The tone the caller took with the three customer service representatives ranged from civil to irate; however, no matter what the tone, no response was received. Of the two companies that did respond, one complaint yielded coupons and recipes in fourteen days, and another phone call (complaint about cereal prices) yielded a lengthy letter explaining cereal pricing (thirteen days), with no coupons or reimbursement. During these phone calls, the consumer asked for some form of reimbursement from only one manufacturer.

Five phone calls sang the products' praises. Two of those phone calls produced coupons. During the remaining three phone calls, the callers requested recipes only. Those recipes have not been received to date.

The results of our experiment show that letters are far more effective in getting coupons or recipes than calling 800 numbers. It is not conclusive whether complaining or praising a product always gets the consumer something from the manufacturer. What is clear, however, is that asking for something works.

What Can You Do If the Manufacturer Doesn't Help?

If you aren't satisfied with the manufacturer's response, the consumer's local office of the FDA or the Better Business Bureau (BBB) may be of help. One FDA public relations specialist noted that, should a consumer write to the FDA about a problem with a product, sending a copy of that letter to the manufacturer helps get their attention. It is also a good idea to include the actual label so that the manufacturer knows which particular product you are referring to. Remember, the FDA will contact the manufacturer or send a warning letter only if there have been several similar complaints or known violations of state and federal laws.

The Better Business Bureau may offer more information. Very concerned consumers may file a complaint in writing, but the bureau advises other preliminary options as well. First, it advises consumers to contact the company again, lay out the situation, and explain what happened. This could be especially useful when dealing with a large company that has enough resources to handle in-depth calls from consumers. The BBB also recommends that consumers seek legal counsel to organize their grievance and to reduce the amount of work required to straighten out confusion. This could mean the difference between a successful, efficient conflict mediation and a costly, slow process in the courts.

The BBB can certainly aid a consumer with its own standard procedures if a complaint is taken up against the product manufacturer. The bureau "doesn't like being ignored," according to one official. If the company puts off either the bureau or the consumer on whose behalf it is working, the bureau is more likely to keep the complaint in the forefront. In the end, a lot depends on the amount of time, energy, and money that the consumer is willing to put in to see the complaint through. When contemplating what steps to take, the BBB, like the FDA, is likely to watch for patterns of complaints regarding the same company or the same product.

It Takes a Lot of Work to Report a Mislabeled Product

What happens when you don't get satisfaction from a retailer or manufacturer about a misleading claim or mislabeled product, and you decide it's time to contact the FDA? According to Janet McDonald of the FDA, here's their procedure:

If a consumer writes a letter to the FDA about a misleading label, the agency probably will not contact the manufacturer or the consumer unless the error is grievous. If the FDA gets a rash of calls about the same product, it will respond, but, McDonald cautions, "What's misleading to one consumer isn't necessarily misleading to all." She said the FDA must set priorities and can't respond to every complaint.

If people want to write letters, a good idea is to include the label of the product and send a letter to the manufacturer with a copy of the letter to the FDA. Still, the FDA won't generally contact a manufacturer unless there's a violation. If that be the case, the first step is a warning letter. The agency follows the normal complaint procedure documented for problem products.

To repeat one of my most important suggestions, contact your supermarket manager and explain the problem to him or her. The manager may handle it directly or refer you to the product buyer at the operations office. The supermarket buyer is one of the most powerful forces in the food industry. If the buyer feels your complaint is justified, you may well see action faster than a speeding bullet. Remember, the supermarket determines what is sold (or not) on its shelves—and its number-one priority is to satisfy and keep shoppers like you.

All in all, it's just one more example of why you and your supermarket manager should become friends.

CHAPTER 7

STORE BRANDS: ARE THEY REALLY A VALUE?

Buying the supermarket's own brand (called a "private label" or "store brand") can save you lots of money, but you have to know what you are buying. Until very recently, store brands have not matched the quality of the national brands.

More of us are relying on store brands than ever before—in fact, these products accounted for about $30 billion in supermarket sales in 1993, an increase of 2 percent over the previous year. That makes the store brand the number-one brand sold in the supermarket. And if we are satisfied with the product, the store's name on the package gives the supermarket chain one more advantage for keeping us as shoppers.

Stores began building their own brands around the turn of the century. Sales of these products grew progressively until television advertising came along and the nationally advertised brands' credibility was tough to compete with. In the early 1970s the recession fueled a resurgence in private labels. Food shoppers needed bargains, so retailers began to offer "generics." These lower- or standard-cost, standard-quality products were often packaged in austere, "minimalist" wrappings that reflected the general retail climate.

Then during the economic upswing of the 1980s, shoppers began turning back to nationally advertised brands. In response, retailers began improving quality and expanding the variety of private-label products. To meet a growing taste for gourmet and specialty foods, retailers even developed "premium" private labels. These products were designed not only to compete with leading brands, but in some cases to surpass the quality and price of national brands.

According to Nielsen Consumer Information Services, the heaviest buyers of private-label products spent an average of $660 on these goods during one year. According to a Gallup poll commissioned by the Private Label Manufacturers Association, "Nearly nine out of every ten respondents, or 86 percent said they have purchased store brands, a level of acceptance that is unparalleled in U.S. consumer history. Store brands can no longer be considered the province of a minority of shoppers."

In a telephone interview, Safeway's John Templeton emphatically told me, "I would put our private label, Safeway Select, up against any national brands or other private label. We provide customers with same or sometimes better quality at comparable or mostly lower prices." He also said that Safeway private-label products are tested by their own quality-assurance experts. The products go through field assurance tests for quality and are tested with outside vendors as well. To sum it all up, Templeton simply stated, "Our private labels are same quality at lower prices."

PUTTING PRIVATE LABELS TO THE TEST

Is it true? I submitted my shopping list of fifty-four items to four of the nation's leading retailers, ShopRite, Jewel, A&P, and Safeway. I asked them to provide me with a cash register receipt showing exactly what I would have to pay if I used their private-label products instead of the name brands. Not one of the stores was able to replace my entire list with its own brand, but the results were outstanding.

The table on the next page compares the price of the total shopping list for national brands with each store's pricing for comparable-quality store-brand products. If no

P RICE C HECK:
N ATIONAL B RANDS VERSUS S TORE B RANDS

Supermarket Chain	National-Brand Market Basket Price	Store-Brand Market Basket Price
A&P	$135.70	$91.13
Jewel	$138.81	$114.36
Safeway	$139.33	$114.71
ShopRite	$135.91	$98.56

store-brand replacement was available, the name brand at its normal price was used.

As you can see, in these four cases you could save considerable dollars if you bought the store's private label. In fact, if you spent approximately this amount each week over a year, you could save over $2,000. (Each geographical area of the country does differ. In the New York area, private-label pricing is the most competitive.)

So you can without a doubt save money by buying store brands, but there are other things to consider before you buy. Quality is the most important. Check the ingredients list to make sure you are comparing same quality. Also check the size of the package. At times store-brand packages are the same size but with a different net weight (usually more). The ultimate test, though, should be taste. Take the time to compare.

I've bought plenty of store-brand products that can't compare with the quality or consistency of brand-name alternatives. So how can we tell which store brands are the best value? The best way is to do your own taste and price comparisons. Make sure that you are comparing like products, though. That goes beyond just weight and size to include the quality of ingredients used. Read the ingredients list carefully, and you might find a few surprises. For example, on pasta sauce, you'll see the first ingredients vary. Some lists begin with tomato puree, some with tomato sauce, some with crushed tomatoes, and some even have water as the first ingredient.

Based on responses from retailers across the country, here are the products and categories that usually offer the best value, quality, and taste. Remember that each chain has its own standards. A store brand in one store is different from that in another. In no particular order, here are the store-brand suggestions to try:

- *"Indulgent-type" cookies*—These are chocolate-chip cookies that promote an extraordinary quantity of chips. Check the ingredients list to see whether flour or chocolate is listed first.
- *Salsa*—Check the ingredients list to make sure the first ingredient is tomatoes.
- *Dairy products*—Besides milk, check out yogurt, cottage cheese, and hard natural cheeses like Swiss and cheddar. To make a fair comparison, look for the amount of aging and the state of origin.
- *Preserves and jams*—These products offer some of the best values and quality in store brands. Look for

the fruit itself to be listed as the first ingredient, rather than fruit juice or a sugar.

■ *Pasta and pasta sauces*—Make sure you read the ingredients list. On the pasta label, look for the country of origin and type of wheat. Sauce ingredients vary—the best will list tomatoes or crushed tomatoes first. Listing tomato paste as the first ingredient tells you that the tomatoes were already cooked once, so some taste and nutrients may be lost.

THE FUTURE?

According to *The Food Institute Report*, private-label programs of large supermarket chains were expected to become larger in 1995. The reason behind this trend is said to be a widening gap between the prices of the identical private-label and branded products. Prices of national-brand products are as much as 20 percent higher than private label on some products, and consumers are increasingly noticing this difference. In a nationwide poll of 1,000 shoppers conducted for *Supermarket News* by America's Research Group, results support retailer reports of increased private-label sales, as well as predictions of continued growth. More than 40 percent of shoppers responded that they were buying more private-label products.

Why are private labels so popular? "Part of it is due to better products and the advent of premium quality," says Wendy Wagner, a spokesperson for the Private Label

Manufacturers Association. "Private labels in general have improved their quality since the last recession. They're packaged more attractively, and there's more product innovation."

I would also like to suggest an even stronger reason. Supermarkets have become proud of their private-label goods. The attention and detail they now spend on their own products equal (and in some cases may exceed) their efforts on brands. Supermarkets are promoting more private-label products with special sales and samplings.

Private-label products can be a good buy but are not necessarily cheaper. As we witness the evolution of the store brand to a better-quality product, the price differential may shrink. In fact, some of the most successful President's Choice and Master's Choice private-label products are higher-priced than the leading brands. So compare, but compare the value, not just the price.

WHAT PRIVATE-LABEL INSIDERS SAY

For an insider's look at the private-label world of supermarkets, we interviewed three of the largest providers of supermarket brands. Here's what we learned from each.

Foodland Distributors, Inc.

Foodland operates stores under the names Food Center, Foodland, and Kessel Food Market. We talked to Sharon Dishaw, Foodland's private-label coordinator.

Q: What are the names of your private-label lines?

A: Nature's Best (upscale, preferred selection), Bi-Rite, and Homebest.

Q: What are the benefits of using private-label products?

A: The qualities of private-label products are now up to the standards of national brands and sometimes even better. They're especially good for the baby boomer generation, which nowadays is more educated and demands more choices. When you look at such items as baby diapers, there are no differences at all. We all have to use the same materials to manufacture them. Many of our private-label products are even manufactured by the same companies that manufacture national brands.

Q: What kinds of programs do you have for quality assurance?

A: There is a quality-assurance lab division at Supervalu Inc. Customers can call or write anytime to complain or express opinions about our private-label products. Also, the store has a follow-up policy. Everything is checked back with the consumers for satisfaction. For example, one customer found an ink spot on our own private-label paper towel. The quality-control lab was notified, and they did a complete follow-up with that customer. She also received coupons for future purchases as an appreciation for her cooperation with the follow-up procedures.

Q: What are your top 10 private-label products?

A: 1. Macaroni and cheese (Nature's Best)
      2. Cookies (Nature's Best)
      3. Apple juice (Nature's Best)

4. Applesauce (Nature's Best)
5. Tomato sauces (Nature's Best)
6. Tea bags (Nature's Best)
7. Ketchup (Nature's Best)
8. Peanut butter (Nature's Best)
9. Cereals (Nature's Best)
10. Diapers (Homebest)

The Great Atlantic & Pacific Tea Company

This company operates the A&P chain of supermarkets. We spoke with Michael Rourke, the company's senior vice president of marketing.

Q: What are your private-label lines?
A: America's Choice (which is comparable to national brands at 30 to 40 percent less), Eight O'Clock, and Master's Choice (upscale, higher quality than national brands).

Q: What are the benefits of using private-label products?
A: The savings and values they bring to the customers. Customers are saving on marketing and packaging costs when they buy private labels. Our traditional private-label line, which is comparable to any national brand, is usually 30 to 40 percent less than the national brands. We also guarantee the quality of all our private-label products.

Q: What kinds of programs do you have for quality assurance?
A: We have consumer tasting tests in the stores. We also have quality-assurance labs. A recent study by the *New York Times* concluded that our diapers stand up to the quality standards of any national brand. We provide cus-

tomers with a satisfaction guarantee policy on all our private labels. We contract out with several different suppliers for quality-assurance programs as well as our own testing lab.

Q: What are your top 10 private-label products?

A: 1. Pasta (Master's Choice)

2. Pasta sauce (Master's Choice)

3. Paper towels (America's Choice)

4. Coffee (Eight O'Clock)

5. Jams (Master's Choice)

6. Soda (Master's Choice)

7. Canned fruits (America's Choice)

8. Canned vegetables (America's Choice)

9. Beauty aids (Health Pride)

10. Cold remedy (Health Pride)

American Stores Inc.

American Stores operates stores under the names Acme, Jewel, Jewel Osco, Lucky, and Star Market. We talked to Diane Maffia, director of public relations for American Stores.

Q: What are the names of your private-label lines?

A: We have a three-tiered program: Valuwise (commodity grade); Acme, Jewel, Osco, Sav-On, LadyLee (store brands); and President's Choice, American Premier (premium, upscale).

Q: What are the benefits of using private-label products?

A: Value! These products allow consumers to save money.

Consumers are receiving the same or sometimes even better quality for comparable or lower prices.

Q: What kinds of programs do you have for quality assurance?
A: There is an overall quality assurance-program, which sets specifications and acts as an ongoing watchdog for all old and new products. Our buyers and quality-assurance people do regular plant visits to assess quality assurance. We also conduct an ongoing cutting program; this is actual sampling of the products in the store or labs. We have warehouse inspections for regular lot samples for product testing.

Q: What are your top 10 private-label products?
A: I don't have the data to identify our top 10 items, but our top 10 categories are:

1. Laundry detergent
2. Household cleaning supplies
3. Paper products
4. Canned fruits
5. Canned vegetables
6. Cereal
7. Dry breakfast foods
8. Cookies
9. Soda pops
10. Frozen foods

CHAPTER 8

READY TO MAKE THE MOST OF YOUR SUPERMARKET SHOPPING?

We started this journey together in the land of the supermarket with the objective of seeing (and shopping) the supermarket differently than before. I hope that we have accomplished that goal. I know from experience that even if you use just half of the ideas and hints I've shared with you, you'll save big bucks and enjoy shopping more.

As we approach the millennium, I truly believe that the supermarket will become a more important centerpiece in our lives. Food companies are producing better-tasting and more healthful foods. Kitchen appliances are becoming simpler to use and have more advanced features. And as I see it, the supermarket is where it all comes together. The supermarket in the year 2000 will be a fabulous gathering of freshness, information, and *value*.

I do hope we will meet—on one of my hundreds of shopping trips, on-line, through fax, phone, or letter. The best I could hope for is that you come up behind me in the supermarket one day, tap me on the shoulder, and ask, "Why did you buy that?"

Until then, here's just one more way to have fun and get value. Good Shopping!

W<small>HO'S THE</small> B<small>EST</small> S<small>HOPPER IN</small> Y<small>OUR</small> F<small>AMILY</small>?: A F<small>UN</small> (<small>AND</small> R<small>EALISTIC</small>) A<small>UDIT</small>

Who really is the best supermarket shopper in your house? If your family is like most I've interviewed, almost everyone thinks he or she is! That is, until the discussion starts about what exactly "best" means.

Are you the shopper who saves the most money? Or buys the best quality? Or shops in the least amount of time? What are the characteristics of today's best shoppers?

On the basis of the thousands of consumers I've met and the countless supermarkets I've visited, here is my supermarket best-shopper profile: The "best shopper" is the one family member who knows the supermarket, looks to save money, understands what's in the products he or she buys, and enjoys the shopping experience.

I guarantee my audit is fun, and it will quite possibly put to rest all future family arguments—or at least give you a few ideas how you can shop better. All you have to do is make enough copies for each shopper in your family, take it with you on your next shopping trip, and fill in the answers as you shop.

Ready?

THE BEST-SHOPPER AUDIT

Time Efficiency

1. Day of the week you normally shop: _____

2. Time to drive to store: _____ × 2 = _____ minutes

3. Time you entered supermarket: _____

4. Time checked out (attach register receipt): _____

5. Total supermarket shopping time: _____

Continued on next page

Shopping Preparation

1. Did you read your supermarket's newspaper ad?
   ☐ yes   ☐ no

2. Did you take it with you to the supermarket?
   ☐ yes   ☐ no

3. Number of coupons you took to the supermarket: _____

4. Total value of coupons: $_____

5. Actual value of coupons redeemed (read off receipt): $_____

6. Total dollar amount (before coupons) of your shopping receipt: $_____

7. Percentage you saved by using coupons: _____%

8. Where do you get your coupons? (Check all that apply.)
   ☐ newspaper   ☐ magazine
   ☐ mailed to your home ☐ in store
   ☐ belong to coupon club ☐ trade with friend
   ☐ other: _____

9. Did you make a shopping list?
   ☐ yes   ☐ no

10. Number of items on your shopping list: _____

11. Actual number of items purchased (count on receipt): _____

The Supermarket

1. Name of the store manager:

   _____

2. How many store employees do you recognize? _____

3. How many recognize you and greet you? _____

4. Do you go up and down the aisles in the entire store?
   ☐ yes   ☐ no

5. Do you shop only aisles where the products on your list are?
   ☐ yes   ☐ no

6. Do you stop and sample products that are being demonstrated?
   ☐ yes   ☐ no

7. Do you ask for a coupon on these products?
   ☐ yes   ☐ no

8. How often do you buy products that you sample the same day?
   ☐ always   ☐ 25% of the time
   ☐ 75% of the time   ☐ never
   ☐ 50% of the time

9. Does the rest of your family like these products?
   ☐ always   ☐ 25% of the time
   ☐ 75% of the time   ☐ never
   ☐ 50% of the time

10. How often do you read the nutritional information on a NEW product?
    ☐ always   ☐ 25% of the time
    ☐ 75% of the time   ☐ never
    ☐ 50% of the time

Continued on next page

11. How often do you read the ingredients list on a NEW product?

☐ always   ☐ 25% of the time

☐ 75% of the time   ☐ never

☐ 50% of the time

Your Home

1. List all the places in your home where you store groceries:

_____

_____

_____

2. Can you see all the items in your cupboard?

☐ yes   ☐ no

3. As you are putting away this shopping trip's groceries, how many of the same products already in your cupboard did you buy? _____

4. How many have been in your cupboard at least 2 months?

_____

5. Can you see all the items in your refrigerator?

☐ yes   ☐ no

6. As you are putting away this shopping trip's groceries, how many of the same products already in your refrigerator did you buy? _____

Reality Check

1. How good a shopper do YOU think you are?

☐ the best   ☐ getting better

☐ great   ☐ I hate to shop

☐ good

2. How good a shopper does the rest of your family think you are? (Ask them!)

☐ the best   ☐ getting better
☐ great   ☐ I hate to shop
☐ good

After your shopping trips, bring home the copies and compare the answers. See who in your family does the best shopping for you.

APPENDIX A

FOOD SAFETY: A SHOPPER'S RESPONSIBILITY

When should you never buy a product? With more supermarkets selling more fresh foods than ever before, it's critical that we understand and practice good food safety. According to the FDA, each year over 40 million Americans become ill from food-borne microorganisms—generally called food poisoning. Can we avoid being one of these victims? Yes, we can, by following some simple guidelines while cooking *and* when shopping in the supermarket.

No one wants to get food poisoning or to expose his or her family to food-borne illnesses, but we do every day. Improper preparation of food at home accounts for almost 30 percent of food poisoning. That leaves our supermarkets, food stores, and restaurants responsible for the other 70 percent.

We can greatly reduce our chances of food-borne illness by following a few simple guidelines. These helpful hints and standards have been collected from the USDA, FDA, and interviews with experts. I have broken these guidelines into the following categories for easy reference:

- Types of food poisoning—their sources, symptoms, and prevention
- When you should never buy a product
- Ways to tell if your supermarket is really clean
- At-home food storage guidelines (including storage temperatures)
- At-home cooking, reheating, and thawing guidelines (including proper cooking temperatures)

Types of Food Poisoning: Sources, Symptoms, and Prevention

According to most of the literature published by the U.S. Department of Agriculture (USDA), a few types of bacteria are responsible for most cases of food-borne illnesses. Food-borne illnesses result from a combination of bacterias naturally present in our environment and food-handling mistakes made in the home, stores, and other commercial settings. These bacterias cannot be seen, smelled, or tasted. Young children, pregnant women, and senior citizens tend to be most susceptible to these bacterias.

Salmonellosis

Sources: Salmonella infections occur when a person ingests salmonella, a type of bacteria found primarily in uncooked poultry, eggs, beef, pork, and other meat, as well as in poultry salads, Mexican food, potato salad, baked goods, macaroni and cheese, and unpasteurized dairy products. Salmonella can also be found in the feces and intestinal tracts of dogs, cats, rodents, and certain turtles and wild animals (*FSIS Facts*, December 1990).

The bacteria is digested and continually reproduces in the small intestine. The numbers increase to such a large amount that the symptoms of salmonella exposure surface. Certain types of salmonella cause illness in humans and animals, while others affect humans only. One of the most common types of bacteria is called *Salmonella enteritidis*. This bacteria is linked to Grade A eggs, and scientists believe that hens carrying the bacteria transfer it to the eggs.

Symptoms: Approximately 40,000 cases of salmonellosis are reported each year (*Preventing Food-Borne Illness*, USDA, September 1990). The symptoms include a sudden onset of fever, gripping and severe abdominal pain, nausea and vomiting, lack of appetite, foul-smelling diarrhea, weakness, and dehydration. It primarily attacks the gastrointestinal system but in extreme cases may invade other areas of the body, causing pneumonia, meningitis, and pericarditis. The illness usually occurs in six to forty-eight hours after exposure and may last from three days to three weeks, depending on the overall condition of the infected person.

Prevention: Tartakow and Vorperian in *Foodborne and Waterborne Diseases* suggest the following measures for prevention of salmonellosis:

- Thoroughly cook all foods from animal sources.
- Avoid eating raw, dirty, or cracked eggs.
- Eat pasteurized milk products.
- Refrigerate prepared foods as well as leftovers during storage before use.

In addition, literature by the FDA and USDA on safe food handling suggests that consumers should avoid contaminating other foods with juices from raw meat or poultry on counters, utensils, hands, cutting boards, or serving plates.

Campylobacteriosis

Sources: Campylobacter jejuni can be found in untreated water, raw poultry and shellfish, and in the intestinal tracts of chickens, turkeys, cattle, pork, sheep, dogs, cats, rodents, monkeys, some wild birds, and some asymptomatic humans. Like salmonella, campylobacter bacteria must be ingested to do harm. A few hundred cells are all that is needed to lead to an infection. The bacteria thrives in low-oxygen refrigerated environments.

Symptoms: Symptoms of campylobacteriosis include fever, headache, and muscle pain followed by bloody diarrhea, abdominal pain, and nausea. The nausea can appear two to ten days after the food has been ingested and remains for approximately one to ten days. Exposure to this bacteria can lead to meningitis, urinary tract infection, and reactive arthritis.

Prevention: Thoroughly cook all meat, poultry, and fish. Wash all utensils, surfaces, and hands that touch raw meat with soap and a fingernail brush or scouring pad. Avoid unpasteurized milk and untreated water.

Staphylococcus aureus (Staph)

Sources: The staph bacteria is found in human skin, infected cuts and pimples, and noses and throats. The bacteria may also be exhaled during conversation, coughing, or sneezing. The bacteria increases in warm temperatures and thrives in foods high in protein. The bacteria also reproduces in foods high in sugar or salt. Food sources include ham, turkey, chicken, pork, roast beef, chicken and turkey salads, potato salads, cream-filled pastry, eggs and egg salad, custard, luncheon meat, hot dogs, and Mexican food.

Symptoms: Symptoms of exposure are nausea, vomiting, diarrhea, occasional fever, chills, headache, weakness, and dizziness. The symptoms occur within thirty minutes to eight hours after ingestion and last from three to five days.

Prevention: Wash hands and utensils before serving food. Refrigerate cooked food in shallow, covered containers to prevent the spread of the bacteria. Thoroughly cook all meats. Do not allow prepared food to sit at room temperature for more than two hours.

Clostridium perfringens

Sources: The *Clostridium perfringens* bacteria is present in soil, sewage, and intestines of humans and animals. The bacteria grows in environments with little or no oxygen in the form of a vegetative cell or spore. The vegetative cell leads to exposure, which causes illness. Although cooking kills the majority of the cells, spores can subsist and produce toxins. The bacteria usually grows in foods served in large quantities or those left at room temperature for an extended period of time.

Symptoms: The symptoms of poisoning with this bacteria include diarrhea and gas pains that appear within nine to fifteen hours after ingestion and persist for about a day.

Prevention: Keep cooked foods hot or cold. Divide large portions of cooked food into smaller serving sizes. Thoroughly reheat leftovers.

Botulism

Sources: Botulism is one of the most deadly food-borne diseases. The illness is a result of the ingestion of *Clostridium botulinum* found in some foods. The toxins can be of four types (Type A, B, E, or F) and survive at temperatures above 38 degrees Fahrenheit.

The bacteria is found in rotting vegetables and forests; the bottoms of streams, lakes, and coastal waters; in crabs and shellfish; in soils from farms; and in feces and carcasses of birds and animals. The bacteria can be found in the following foods: peppers and pepper sauce, asparagus, beans (green, lima, salad, soy), salmon and fish eggs, tomatoes and tomato juice, other juice, beets, improperly fermented fish, pickles/relish, and baked potatoes and potato salad. Meat loaf, pot pie, and stew left at room temperature overnight also harbor the bacteria.

Symptoms: Botulism affects the nervous system. Initially, someone affected with botulism suffers from dry mouth, double vision, difficulty focusing on a near point, and difficulty swallowing. Symptoms also include nausea, vomiting, abdominal cramps, diarrhea, sore throat, dizziness, constipation, weakness, muscle paralysis, and difficulty breathing. These symptoms can occur twelve to forty-eight hours after food ingestion, but symptoms may be delayed for as long as eight days. These symptoms last one to ten days.

Prevention: Do not eat food from containers with leaking or bulging lids or from containers that have been damaged. Avoid canned foods that have strange odors or appearances. Refrigerate food in covered, shallow containers within two hours after serving. Reheat all refrigerated food thoroughly. Divide large portions of cooked foods into smaller portions for serving.

Listeria monocytogenes

Sources: The *Listeria monocytogenes* bacteria is found in the intestines of humans and animals and in milk, soil, leafy vegetables, and food-processing environments. Soft-ripened and pasteurized cheeses, milk, ice cream, raw and processed meat, raw and cooked seafood, precut and packaged vegetables can also harbor the bacteria. In certain foods, the bacteria can double in one to two days if kept at 39 degrees Fahrenheit.

Symptoms: Symptoms include sudden onset of flulike symptoms, such as fever, chills, headache, backache, abdominal pain, and diarrhea. In newborn infants the symptoms include respiratory distress, refusal to drink, early discharge of meconium, skin nodules in the throat or on the back, and vomiting. Listeriosis can cause spontaneous abortions (miscarriages) or stillbirths. Elderly people may also suffer from meningitis or other complications.

Prevention: Avoid dairy products made from unpasteurized milk. Observe and abide by food expiration dates. Thoroughly reheat frozen or refrigerated meat and poultry products.

Escherichia coli

Sources: The *Escherichia coli (E. coli)* bacteria is frequently found in contaminated water. Raw or rare beef and unpasteurized milk also lead to illness associated with this bacteria. *E. coli* attacks the intestinal tract. It can also be transmitted person to person. The bacteria typically grows at temperatures of 44 degrees Fahrenheit or higher.

Symptoms: The major symptoms are abdominal cramps followed by bloody diarrhea, nausea, vomiting, and a fever. Although few complications are related to *E. coli,* the most common is hemolytic uremic syndrome—a urinary tract infection that can cause acute kidney failure, brain damage, strokes, and seizures in children and the elderly.

The symptoms begin three to four days after the food has been ingested and can last up to ten days.

Prevention: Thoroughly cook all food. Prepare and store food in sanitary environments. Refrigerate food at 40 degrees Fahrenheit or below.

Yersinia enterocolitica

Sources: The *Yersinia enterocolitica* bacteria is found in pigs and pig waste. In terms of food, the bacteria thrives in chocolate milk, white milk, other dairy products, mussels, tofu, oysters, and contaminated water.

Symptoms: The symptoms are abdominal pain, fever, diarrhea, and vomiting. The symptoms begin within one to seven days after consumption and last for one to two days. Complications include arthritic or anemic conditions, thyroid disease, acute carditis, and meningitis.

Prevention: The best prevention is thorough cooking and reheating of food, as well as good sanitation and personal hygiene.

What to Do If You Suspect Food Poisoning

If you suspect that you might be suffering from a foodborne illness, there are several measures to take. First of all, act like a detective and preserve all the evidence. If you suspect that a certain food has made you ill, try to write down everything about that particular food or dish (the ingredients, when it was made, when you ate it, where it was purchased, when you first exhibited signs of illness). This evidence might be very useful to health and/or medical officials in tracking the problem.

Second, seek treatment for the illness if it seems necessary. While the person is ill, it is vital that he or she remain hydrated. The sick person should consume as many liquids as possible to replace fluids lost from diarrhea and/or vomiting. If the victim is young, pregnant, or elderly, seek medical attention quickly.

Lastly, call your local health department if the food was served at a large gathering (as in the case of a restaurant or catered banquet) or if the food was from a restaurant or other type of commercial setting, was prepared in a supermarket, or was a commercial product. If the illness is a result of USDA-inspected food products, call the meat and poultry hotline at (800) 535-4555 or your local FDA office.

Ten Signs That Tell You When You Should Never Buy a Product

Of course, it's best to avoid food poisoning in the first place. Any of the following signs can alert you to problems that may mean a product is defective, spoiled, or has been mishandled:

1. Don't buy foods in dented, rusty, bulging, or leaky cans or any package with a broken seal.
2. Don't buy already cracked or nonrefrigerated eggs. Buy and store eggs in their original carton.
3. Don't buy foods that do not hold up to standard when you inspect them by sight, smell, or touch.
4. Check the "buy by" or "sell by" dates. Never buy foods past the expiration date.
5. Avoid meat and chicken, or anything *prewrapped*, that has been wrapped improperly and is leaking.
6. Refuse to buy *just-wrapped* deli or seafood items that have been wrapped carelessly, exposing the food to your touch and to bacteria that may be present on the deli counter, scale, or utensils.
7. Check the cleanliness of the department and its employees. Don't buy if employees are handling food without gloves on or if their gloves and aprons are dirty.
8. Check thermostats in refrigerated or frozen-food display cases. Don't buy anything in refrigerators whose temperature exceeds 40 degrees Fahrenheit or in freezers above 0 degrees Fahrenheit. Don't buy frozen foods stocked above the freezer line.
9. Don't buy any foods requiring proper storage that are allowed to sit out at room temperature to spoil or attract bacteria, or where flies or other insects in the supermarket can get at them.
10. Never accept fish that is loosely packaged or wrapped in waxed or deli paper. If you will not be using or refrigerating it within twenty minutes, request that fish be sealed in a plastic bag and placed in another plastic bag of ice to ensure freshness and safety.

TEN WAYS TO TELL IF YOUR SUPERMARKET IS *REALLY* CLEAN

Is your supermarket clean enough to prevent the spread of food-borne illness? Look for this evidence:

1. Are the shopping carts clean? Odd pieces of foods, beverages, produce, and meats from spills or poorly wrapped products can contaminate the foods you buy.

2. Bathroom cleanliness is a good indication of employee and store practices, as well as management's seriousness about sanitation.

3. Look for frequently changed aprons and handling gloves.

4. You should never find spattered blood on display cases, ceilings, or other areas.

5. Check out the food cases. Are crumbs, loose food, and dirt collecting in the corners? If your store sells bulk foods, make sure they are sold in either plastic cases or wood cases with plastic liners. Nuts, grains, and other bulk foods can be a breeding ground for insects and rodents.

6. Look at "sell by" and freshness dates. Sometimes they can be altered. If you have any question, immediately bring it to the attention of the store manager—not the department manager.

7. Read the local newspapers. In most cities, these list any food establishments that are in violation of the law (or have received warnings) for unsanitary conditions.

8. Ask your store manager who inspects the store. If you are at all concerned, ask for a copy of the inspection record.

9. Take a look behind the supermarket, in the back where deliveries are received. Is it clean? Where is the Dumpster? Is it covered and away from the store?

10. Even the checkout lane should be clean. Remember that fresh or uncooked items such as produce can contaminate other products while waiting to be packed.

At-Home Food Storage Guidelines

Once you bring your food home, you are responsible for handling it safely. Follow these guidelines for storing your food:

- Keep hot foods hot, cold foods cold.
- Store foods (well wrapped) in the refrigerator. Make sure they are tightly wrapped and don't leak.
- Check labels for individual food storage directions—and follow them!
- Don't overstuff your fridge. That prevents air circulation.

- Don't let cooked foods sit around at room temperature for more than two hours.
- Keep newly bought poultry or meat in the refrigerator for no more than two days.
- Store hot leftovers in small, shallow containers. This hastens cooling; if foods cool too slowly, bacteria can grow fast.
- Refrigerate leftovers ASAP and eat them within three days.
- For picnics or sack lunches, store food with cold packs. Keep lids shut and bags closed up.
- Always maintain a clean refrigerator and freezer. Wash with warm soap and water regularly.

Time Limits for Food Storage

Product	Refrigerator (40° F)	Freezer (0° F)
Eggs		
Fresh, in shell	3 weeks	Don't freeze
Raw yolks, whites	2–4 days	1 year
Hard cooked	1 week	Don't freeze well
Liquid pasteurized eggs or egg substitutes		
Opened:	3 days	Don't freeze
Unopened:	10 days	1 year

Product	Refrigerator (40° F)	Freezer (0° F)

Mayonnaise

Refrigerate after opening	2 months	Don't freeze

TV Dinners, Frozen Entrees

Keep frozen until ready to serve	Don't refrigerate	3–4 months

Deli and Vacuum-Packed Products

Store-prepared (or homemade) egg, chicken, tuna, ham, and macaroni salads	3–5 days	These products don't freeze well.
Prestuffed pork and lamb chops, chicken breasts stuffed with dressing	1 day	
Store-cooked convenience meals	1–2 days	
Commercial brand vacuum-packed dinners with USDA seal unopened	2 weeks	

Soups and Stews

Vegetable or meat-added	3–4 days	2–3 months

Continued on next page

Product	Refrigerator (40° F)	Freezer (0° F)

Hamburger, Ground and Stew Meats

Hamburger and stew meats	1–2 days	3–4 months
Ground turkey, veal, pork, lamb and mixtures of them	1–2 days	3–4 months

Hot Dogs and Lunch Meats

Hot dogs, opened package	1 week	In freezer wrap: 1–2 months
Hot dogs, unopened package	2 weeks	
Lunch meats, opened	3–5 days	
Lunch meats, unopened	2 weeks	

Bacon and Sausage

Bacon	7 days	1 month
Sausage, raw, from pork, beef, turkey	1–2 days	1–2 months
Smoked breakfast links, patties	7 days	1–2 months
Hard sausage— pepperoni, jerky sticks	2–3 weeks	1–2 months

Ham, Corned Beef

Corned beef, drained, wrapped in pouch with pickling juices	5–7 days	1 month

Product	Refrigerator (40° F)	Freezer (0° F)
Ham, canned, label says keep refrigerated	6–9 months	Don't freeze
Ham, fully cooked, whole	7 days	1–2 months
Ham, fully cooked, half	3–5 days	1–2 months
Ham, fully cooked, slices	3–4 days	1–2 months

Fresh Meats

Steaks, beef	3–5 days	6–12 months
Chops, pork	3–5 days	4–6 months
Chops, lamb	3–5 days	6–9 months
Roasts, beef	3–5 days	6–12 months
Roasts, pork and veal	3–5 days	4–6 months
Variety meats—tongue, brain, kidney, liver, heart, chitterlings	1–2 days	3–4 months

Leftover Meat

Cooked meat and meat dishes	3–4 days	2–3 months
Gravy and meat broth	1–2 days	2–3 months

Fresh Poultry

Chicken or turkey, whole	1–2 days	1 year

Continued on next page

Product	Refrigerator (40° F)	Freezer (0° F)
Chicken or turkey pieces	1–2 days	9 months
Giblets	1–2 days	3–4 months
Cooked Poultry, Leftover		
Fried chicken	3–4 days	4 months
Cooked poultry dishes	3–4 days	4–6 months
Pieces, plain	3–4 days	4 months
Pieces covered with broth, gravy	1–2 days	6 months
Chicken nuggets, patties	1–2 days	1–3 months

AT-HOME COOKING, REHEATING, AND THAWING GUIDELINES

Always keep your preparation areas clean—and that includes you, too! Keep hair back, and wash your hands in warm water with soap (especially after smoking, using the bathroom, and handling different foods).

1. Keep your refrigerator clean. Throw out old food and keep cooked and raw food separate. Check the refrigerator temperature occasionally. The main part should

not be more than 40 degrees Fahrenheit, and the freezer not above 0 degrees Fahrenheit.

2. Use clean utensils washed in soap and water, and wash them again afterward. Also wash cutting boards, counters, and can openers frequently.

3. Never put cooked food on plates that previously held raw meat, poultry, fish, or seafood.

4. You can't always smell harmful bacteria. Don't even think you can!

Always follow the proper cooking temperatures. The following table summarizes temperatures to which meat, poultry, and other products should be heated when you cook them.

Always reheat foods to at least 165 degrees Fahrenheit. Never thaw at room temperature. Safe ways to thaw are:

■ In the microwave oven
■ In the refrigerator
■ In a bath of ice cubes in the sink
■ While cooking the food
■ Under cold, running water

If you marinate meats, do so in the refrigerator.

If you use a microwave, follow these safety tips:

■ Cover food with a lid or plastic wrap so steam can aid thorough cooking. Vent the wrap and make sure it doesn't touch the food.

■ Stir and rotate your food for even cooking. No turntable? Rotate the dish by hand once or twice during cooking.

■ Observe the standing time called for in a recipe or cooking directions. Microwave cooking is based on vibrating atoms and molecules, which do not stop just because the food is removed from the oven. During the standing time, the food finishes cooking.

■ Use an oven temperature probe or a meat thermometer to check that food is done. Be sure to insert it at several spots.

Proper Cooking Temperatures and Times

Product	Safe Temperature or Cooking Time

Eggs and Egg Dishes

Eggs	Cook until yolk and white are firm
Egg dishes	160°F

Ground Meat and Meat Mixtures

Turkey, chicken	170°F
Veal, beef, lamb, pork	160°F

Fresh Beef

Rare (some bacterial risk)	140°F
Medium	160°F
Well done	170°F

Fresh Veal

Medium	160°F
Well done	170°F

Product	Safe Temperature or Cooking Time
Fresh Lamb	
Medium	160°F
Well done	170°F
Fresh Pork	
Medium	160°F
Well done	170°F
Poultry	
Chicken, whole	180°F
Turkey, whole	180°F
Poultry breasts, roasts	170°F
Poultry thighs, wings	Cook until juices run clear
Stuffing (cooked alone or in bird)	165°F
Duck and goose	180°F
Ham	
Fresh (raw)	160°F
Precooked (to reheat)	140°F
Seafood	
Shrimp	5 min. boiling
Fish	Till flaky
Clams	5–10 min. steamed
Oysters	5 min.

Glossary of Food Additives and Preservatives

additive: Any substance that becomes part of a food product when added either intentionally to produce a desired effect or unintentionally through processing, storage, or packaging.

amino acids: Compounds needed by the body in a certain combination. Animal protein usually has the needed composition, but the acids may be used to fortify vegetables and bring them close to the needed levels.

anticaking agents: Chemicals like silicon dioxide, calcium silicate, and iron ammonium citrate, added to powdered foods to prevent clumping.

BHA (butylated hydroxyanisole): *See* BHT.

BHT (butylated hydroxytoluene): Like BHA, a preservative that blocks oxidation in fats and oils, preventing rancidity. BHA and BHT are also used in snacks, cereals, and instant potatoes.

B vitamins: Niacin, thiamine, and riboflavin; vitamins added to or used to enrich bread, flour, and cereals to help combat nutritional deficiencies.

D&C: Prefix meaning that a dye is FDA-approved for drugs and cosmetics.

emulsifier: An additive used in the preparation and processing of foods, used to blend or mix ingredients together and keep them from separating.

Ext. D&C: Prefix signifying a dye is FDA-approved for externally applied drugs and cosmetics only.

FD&C: Prefix meaning a dye is FDA-approved for foods, drugs, and cosmetics.

glycerine: Additive used to retain moisture and keep marshmallows and soft candies soft.

iodine: Mineral added to salt to prevent goiter, an iodine-deficiency disease.

iron: Mineral added to foods to help prevent anemia and other iron-deficiency diseases.

lecithin: Emulsifier, or mixing agent, that helps fat and water stay together. Lecithin is present in egg yolks and milk and so aids mixing in mayonnaise and ice cream.

mono- and diglycerides: Emulsifiers present in bread, margarine, and peanut butter.

MSG (monosodium glutamate): Flavor enhancer derived from beet sugar. MSG is found in some prepared foods and is widely used in restaurants. In some people it causes a reaction known as "Chinese restaurant syndrome," consisting of a tightness in the chest, a burning feeling in the neck and forearms, and a headache. This syndrome usually ceases without the need for medical attention.

nitrites: Chemicals used in combination with salt to impede the growth of the bacterial spores that cause botulism. Nitrites are also used as preservatives and flavor and color enhancers.

preservative: Additive that helps maintain a food's freshness and keeps it from spoiling or oxidizing.

Red #3: Dye whose use in foods may be banned in the near future because of health concerns.

Red #40: Most common food dye.

sorbitol: Sweetener that also helps retain moisture.

sulfites: Antioxidants used primarily to prevent discoloration in dried fruits and other preserved products and to retard bacteria growth in wine. A few people may react adversely to sulfites, with problems varying from difficulty breathing to hives to stomachache to anaphylactic shock. Sulfite-sensitive people should avoid foods whose labels list the sulfites sulfur dioxide, sodium sulfite, sodium or potassium bisulfite, and sodium or potassium metabisulfite.

vitamin D: Vitamin commonly used as an additive to milk. This enrichment has helped prevent the childhood bone disease known as rickets, which was caused by a vitamin D deficiency.

Yellow #5: Second most common food dye. In a few people, Yellow #5 may cause itching or hives. It is listed on labels so that sensitive people can avoid it.

FOOD SAFETY
BIBLIOGRAPHY

Blumenthal, Dale. "Red #3 and Other Colorful Controversies," *FDA Consumer,* 1990.

Blumenthal, Dale and Chris Lecos. "Reacting to Sulfites," *FDA Consumer,* 1985–1986.

"Fishing for Facts on Seafood Safety," under Food-Borne Illness, Food Science and Nutrition Information, on the International Food Information Council Home Page.

Foulke, Judith E. "A Fresh Look at Food Preservatives," *FDA Consumer,* 1993.

Hadfield, Linda C. "How to Avoid Food That Makes You Sick," *Current Health Journal* (March 1995).

Hecht, Annabel. "Preventing Food-Borne Illness," *Consumer Research Reprint,* vol. 25, no. 1 (January 1991).

Henkel, John. "From Shampoo to Cereal," *FDA Consumer,* 1993.

Lehman, Phyllis. "More than You Ever Thought You Would Know About Food Additives," *FDA Consumer,* 1984.

Miller, Roger W. "Mother Nature's Regulations on Food Safety," *Consumer Research Reprint,* vol. 22, no. 3 (April 1988).

"A Quick Consumer Guide to Safe Food Handling," *Home and Garden Bulletin,* no. 248 (September 1990).

Thompson, Dennis. State of California Department of Food and Agriculture, Meat Inspection Division. Personal interview (August 1995).

U.S. Department of Health and Human Services. *An FDA Consumer Memo.* Wasington, D.C.: U.S. Government Printing Office, May 1993.

APPENDIX B

USEFUL ADDRESSES AND PHONE NUMBERS

MANUFACTURERS

Airwick Industries
   1655 Valley Rd.
   Wayne, NJ 07470
   (201) 633-6700

Alberto-Culver Co.
   2525 Armitage Ave.
   Melrose Park, IL 60160
   (708) 450-3000

American Home Foods
685 Third Ave.
New York, NY 10017
(212) 878-6300

Armour Swift-Eckrich
2001 Butterfield Rd.
Downers Grove, IL 60515
(708) 512-1000

Beatrice Cos. Inc.
2 N. LaSalle St.
Chicago, IL 60602
(312) 558-4000

Beech-Nut Nutrition Corp.
Checkerboard Sq.
St. Louis, MO 63164
(314) 982-1679

Best Foods Baking Group
100 Passaic Ave.
Fairfield, NJ 07004
(201) 808-3000

Borden Inc.
180 E. Broad St.
Columbus, OH 43215
(614) 225-4511

Boyle-Midway
685 Third Ave.
New York, NY 10017
(212) 986-1000

Bristol Myers Squibb Co.
345 Park Ave.
New York, NY 10154
(212) 546-4000

Buitoni Foods Corp.
800 N. Brand Blvd.
Glendale, CA 91203
(818) 549-6000

C&C Cola Co. Inc.
535 Dowd Ave.
Elizabeth, NJ 07201
(908) 289-4600

Campbell Soup Co.
Campbell Pl.
Camden, NJ 08103-1700
(609) 342-4800

Chesebrough-Pond's Inc.
33 Benedict Pl.
Greenwich, CT 06830
(203) 661-2000 or
(800) 243-5300

Clairol Inc.
345 Park Ave.
New York, NY 10154
(212) 546-2775 or
(800) 223-5800

Clorox Co.
1221 Broadway
Oakland, CA 94612-1888
(510) 271-7000

The Coca-Cola Co.
Drawer 1734
Atlanta, GA 30301
(404) 676-2121

Colgate-Palmolive Co.
300 Park Ave.
New York, NY 10022
(212) 310-2000 or
(800) 221-4607

Continental Baking Co.
Checkerboard Sq.
St. Louis, MO 63164-0001
(314) 982-4700

CPC International Inc.
Box 8000
Englewood Cliffs, NJ 07632
(201) 894-4000

The Creamette Co.
482 N. First St.
Minneapolis, MN 55401
(612) 333-4281

Del Monte Corp.
Box 193575
San Francisco, CA 94119
(415) 442-4000

Dole Foods Co.
31355 Oak Crest Dr.
W. Lake Village, CA 91361
(818) 879-6600

Dowbrands
Box 68511
Indianapolis, IN 46268
(317) 873-7000 or
(800) 428-4795

The Drackett Co.
201 E. Fourth St.
Cincinnati, OH 45202
(413) 632-1800

Durkee Foods
1655 Valley Rd.
Wayne, NJ 07470
(201) 633-6800

Entenmann's
1724 Fifth Ave.
Bay Shore, NY 11706
(516) 273-6000 or
(800) 832-1440

Fisons Corp.
755 Jefferson Rd.
Rochester, NY 14623
(716) 475-9000 or
(800) 235-5535

Frito-Lay Inc.
Box 66034
Dallas, TX 75266-0634
(214) 351-7000 or
(800) 352-4477

General Foods
250 North St.
White Plains, NY 10625
(914) 335-2500 or
(800) 431-1003

General Mills Inc.
Box 1113
Minneapolis, MN 55440
(612) 540-2311

Gerber Products Co.
445 State St.
Fremont, MI 49413
(616) 928-2000

The Gillette Co.
Prudential Tower Bldg.
Boston, MA 02199
(617) 421-7000

Green Giant Co.
Pillsbury Ctr.
200 S. Sixth St.
Minneapolis, MN 55402
(612) 330-4966 or
(800) 767-4466

Greyhound-Dial Corp.
Dial Tower,
Dial Corp. Ctr.
Phoenix, AZ 85077
(602) 207-2800

H. J. Heinz Co.
Box 57
Pittsburgh, PA 15230-0057
(412) 456-6128

Hershey Chocolate USA
19 E. Chocolate Ave.
Hershey, PA 17033
(717) 534-4200 or
(800) 233-2145

H. P. Hood & Sons Inc.
500 Rutherford Ave.
Boston, MA 02129
(617) 242-0600

Geo. A. Hormel & Co.
501 16th Ave. NE
Austin, MN 55912
(507) 437-5611

Hunt-Wesson Inc.
1645 W. Valencia Dr.
Fullerton, CA 92633
(714) 680-1000

The Andrew Jergens Co.
2535 Spring Grove,
Box 145444
Cincinnati, OH 45214
(513) 632-7744 or
(800) 222-3533

Johnson & Johnson
501 George St.
New Brunswick, NJ 08903
(201) 524-0400 or
(800) 526-2433

Keebler Co.
1 Hollow Tree Lane
Elmhurst, IL 60126
(708) 833-2900

The Kellogg Co.
1 Kellogg Sq.,
Box 3599
Battle Creek, MI 49016-3599
(616) 961-2000

Kimberly-Clark Corp.
401 N. Lake St.
Neenah, WI 54956
(414) 721-2000

Kraft USA
Kraft Court
Glenview, IL 60025
(847) 998-2922 or
(800) 323-0768

Land O'Lakes Inc.
Box 116
Minneapolis,
MN 55440-0116
(612) 481-2222

L'eggs Products Inc.
  Box 2495
  Winston-Salem, NC 27012
  (919) 768-9540

Lender's Bagel Bakery
  450 Island Lane
  West Haven, CT 06516
  (203) 934-9231

Lever Bros. Co. Inc.
  390 Park Ave.
  New York, NY 10022
  (212) 688-6000 or
  (800) 223-0392

Thomas J. Lipton Inc.
  800 Sylvan Ave.
  Englewood Cliffs, NJ 07632
  (201) 567-8000

M&M/Mars Inc. (Corporate)
  6885 Elm St.
  McLean, VA 22101
  (703) 821-4900

McCormick & Co. Inc.
  18 Loveton Circle, Box 6000
  Sparks, MD 21152-6000
  (410) 527-6000 or
  (800) 331-3833

McNeil Consumer Products Co.
  7050 Camp Hill Rd.
  Fort Washington, PA 19034
  (215) 233-7000 or
  (800) 225-8263

Miles Inc.
  1127 Myrtle St.
  Elkhart, IN 46514
  (219) 264-8716

Mobil Chemical Co.
  Consumer Products
  1159 Pittsford Victor Rd.
  Pittsford, NY 14534
  (716) 248-5700

John Morrell & Co.
  250 E. Fifth St.
  Cincinnati, OH 45202
  (513) 852-3500

Morton International Inc.
  Morton Salt Division
  100 N. Riverside Plaza
  Chicago, IL 60606
  (312) 807-2000

Mrs. Paul's Kitchens
  5501 Tabor Rd.
  Philadelphia, PA 19120
  (215) 535-1151

Nabisco Brands Inc.
  100 Deforest
  E. Hanover, NJ 07936
  (201) 503-2000 or
  (800) 223-1049

Nestlé Beverage Co.
  345 Spear St.
  San Francisco, CA 94105
  (415) 546-4600 or
  (800) 637-8531

Nestlé Food Company
  800 N. Brand Blvd.
  Glendale, CA 91203
  (818) 549-6000

Noxell Corp.
11050 York Rd.
Hunt Valley, MD 21030
(410) 785-7300 or
(800) 638-6204

Ore-Ida Foods Inc.
Box 10
Boise, ID 83707
(208) 383-6100

Oscar Mayer Foods Corp.
910 Mayer Ave.
Madison, WI 53704-4287
(608) 241-3311

Pepsi-Cola Co.
1 Pepsi Way
Somers, NY 10589
(914) 767-6000 or
(800) 237-3774

Pet Inc.
Box 393
St. Louis, MO 63166
(314) 622-7700 or
(800) 325-7130

The Pillsbury Co.
Pillsbury Ctr.
200 S. Sixth St.
Minneapolis,
MN 55402-1464
(612) 330-4966 or
(800) 767-4466

Playtex Marketing Corp.
708 Third Ave.
New York, NY 10017
(212) 953-4304

Procter & Gamble Co.
Box 599
Cincinnati, OH 45201
(513) 983-1100 or
(800) 543-7270

The Quaker Oats Co.
Box 9003-049001
Chicago, IL 60604-9001
(312) 222-7111

Ralston Purina Co.
Checkerboard Sq.
St. Louis, MO 63164
(314) 982-1000 or
(800) 345-5678

Revlon Inc.
625 Madison Ave.
New York, NY 10022
(212) 527-4000

Richardson-Vicks USA
1 Far Mill Crossing
Shelton, CT 06484
(203) 925-6000

Riviana Foods Inc.
Box 2636
Houston, TX 77252
(713) 529-3251

RJR Foods Inc.
1301 Ave. of the Americas
New York, NY 10019
(212) 258-5600

Sara Lee Corp.
3 First National Plaza Bldg.
70 W. Madison St.
Chicago, IL 60602
(312) 726-2600

Scott Paper Co.
 Scott Plaza
 Philadelphia, PA 19113
 (215) 522-5000

Smithkline Beecham
 Consumer Products Division
 100 Beecham Dr.
 Pittsburgh, PA 15205
 (412) 928-1000

The J. M. Smucker Co.
 Strawberry Lane
 Orville, OH 44667
 (216) 682-0015

Starkist Foods Inc.
 180 E. Ocean Blvd.
 Long Beach, CA 90802
 (213) 590-7900

Sterling Winthrop
 90 Park Ave.
 New York, NY 10016
 (212) 907-2000

Stouffer Foods Corp.
 30003 Bainbridge Rd.
 Solon, OH 44139
 (216) 248-3600 or
 (800) 225-1180

Tetley Inc.
 100 Commerce Dr.
 Shelton, CT 06484
 (203) 929-9200

Treesweet Products Co.
 16825 Northchase St.,
 Suite 1600
 Houston, TX 77060
 (713) 876-3759

Tree Top Inc.
 Box 248
 Selah, WA 98942
 (509) 697-7251

Tropicana Products Inc.
 Box 338
 Bradenton, FL 34206
 (813) 747-4461 or
 (800) 237-9611

Tyson Foods Inc.
 Box 2020
 Springdale, AR 72765
 (501) 756-4000

Uncle Ben's Inc.
 Box 1752
 5721 Harvey Wilson Dr.
 Houston, TX 77251
 (713) 674-9484

Van Den Berg Foods Co.
 21 Third St. NW
 Madelia, MN 56062
 (507) 642-3323

Vlasic Foods Inc.
 26777 Halstead Rd. #100
 Farmington Hills,
 MI 48331-3541
 (313) 473-2305

Warner-Lambert Co.
 201 Tabor Rd.
 Morris Plains, NJ 07950
 (201) 540-2000 or
 (800) 223-0182

Weight Watchers
International Inc.
519 N. Broadway
Jericho, NY 11753
(516) 943-0400 or
(800) 333-3000

Welch Foods Inc.
100 Main St.
Concord, MA 01742
(508) 371-1000

Wilson Foods Corp.
2601 Northwest Expressway,
Suite 1000 W
Oklahoma City, OK 73112
(405) 879-5500

Consumer Groups

American Council on Science
and Health
1995 Broadway, 2nd Floor
New York, NY 10023-5860
(212) 362-7044

Center for Science in the
Public Interest (CSPI)
1875 Connecticut Ave., NW,
Suite 300
Washington, DC 20009-5728
(202) 332-9110

Community Nutrition Institute
910 17th St., NW, Suite 413
Washington, DC 20006
(202) 776-0595

Consumer Action
116 New Montgomery St.,
Suite 223
San Francisco, CA 94105
(415) 777-9648

Consumer Federation of
America
1424 16th St., NW,
Suite 604
Washington, DC 20036
(202) 387-6121

Consumer Product Safety
Commission
Washington, DC 20207
(800) 638-2772

Consumers Union
101 Truman Ave.
Yonkers, NY 10703-1057
(914) 378-2000

Food Research Action Center
1319 F St., NW
Washington, DC 20004
(202) 393-5060

Healthy People 2000
Office of Disease Prevention
and Health Promotion
U.S. Public Health Service
330 C St., SW, Room 2132
Washington, DC 20201
(202) 205-5963

Institute for Food and
Development Policy/Food First
145 9th St.
San Francisco, CA 94103
(415) 864-8555

National Consumer's League
1701 K St., NW, Suite 1200
Washington, DC 20006
(202) 835-3323

Public Citizen Health
Research Group
2000 P St., NW, Suite 700
Washington, DC 20036
(202) 588-1000

Public Voice for Food and
Health Policy
1101 14th St., NW, Suite 710
Washington, DC 20005
(202) 371-1840

U.S. Office of Consumer Affairs
Consumer Information Center
Pueblo, CO 81009
(303) 866-5189

U.S. Public Interest
Research Group
215 Pennsylvania Ave., SE
Washington, DC 20003
(202) 546-9707

FOOD TRADE
ASSOCIATIONS

American Butter Institute
888 16th St., NW,
2nd Floor
Washington, DC 20006
(202) 296-4250

American Cheese Society
c/o Food Work
34 Downing St.
New York, NY 10014
(212) 727-7939

American Dairy Association
O'Hare International Ctr.
10255 W. Higgins Rd.,
Suite 900
Rosemont, IL 60018-5616
(847) 803-2000

American Dairy Products
Institute
130 N. Franklin St.
Chicago, IL 60606
(312) 782-4888

American Frozen Food Institute
1764 Old Meadow Lane,
Suite 350
McLean, VA 22102
(703) 821-0770

American Producers of Italian
Type Cheese Association
c/o Wisconsin Cheese
Making Association
P.O. Box 2133
Madison, WI 53701
(800) 999-2454

American Association of Meat
Processors
P.O. Box 269
Elizabethtown, PA 17022
(717) 367-1168

American Meat Institute
P.O. Box 3556
Washington, DC 20007
(703) 841-2400

American Seafood Distributors
Association
1525 Wilson Blvd.,
Suite 500
Roslyn, VA 22209
(703) 524-8880

American Shrimp Processor
Association
P.O. Box 50774
New Orleans, LA 70150
(504) 368-1571

American Spice Trade
Association
P.O. Box 1267
Englewood Cliffs, NJ 07632
(201) 568-2163

American Sugar Alliance
1225 Eye St., NW, Suite 905
Washington, DC 20005
(202) 457-1457

American Wholesale Marketers
Association
1128 16th St.
Washington, DC 20036
(202) 463-2124

Association for Dressing &
Sauces
5225 Peachtree-Dunwoody Rd.
Suite 500-G
Atlanta, GA 30342
(404) 252-3663

Beverage Network
4437 Concord Lane
Skokie, IL 60076
(847) 673-4614

Calorie Control Council
  5225 Peachtree-Dunwoody Rd.
  Suite 5005-G
  Atlanta, GA 30342
  (404) 252-3663

Canned & Cooked Meat
Importers Association
  1215 17th St., NW
  Washington, DC 20036
  (202) 887-0353

Canned Food Information
Council
  500 N. Michigan Ave.,
  Suite 300
  Chicago, IL 60611
  (312) 836-7279

Canned Fruit Promotion Service
  P.O. Box 7111
  San Francisco, CA 94120
  (415) 495-7714

Cheese Importers Association of
America
  460 Park Ave.
  New York, NY 10022
  (212) 753-7500

Chocolate Manufacturers
Association
  7900 Westpark Dr.,
  Suite A-320
  McLean, VA 22102
  (703) 790-5011

Corn Refiners Association
  1201 Pennsylvania Ave., NW,
  Suite 950
  Washington, DC 20006
  (202) 337-1634

Dairy Industry Committee
  6245 Executive Blvd.
  Rockville, MD 20852
  (301) 984-1444

Dairy Research Foundation
  95 King St.
  Elk Grove Village, IL 60007
  (847) 228-7742

Distilled Spirits Council of the
United States
  1250 Eye St., NW, Suite 900
  Washington, DC 20005
  (202) 628-3544

Flavor & Extract Manufacturers
Association
  1620 Eye St., NW, Suite 925
  Washington, DC 20006
  (202) 293-5800

Food & Drug Law Institute
  1000 Vermont Ave.,
  12th Floor
  Washington, DC 20005
  (202) 371-1420

Food Marketing Institute
  800 Connecticut Ave., NW
  Washington, DC 20006
  (202) 452-8444

Food Service & Packaging
Institute
  1901 N. Mooer St., No. 1141
  Arlington, VA 22209
  (703) 527-7505

Food Service Marketing
Institute
  339 Main St.
  Lake Placid, NY 12946
  (518) 523-2942

Frozen Vegetable Council
  1838 El Camino Real,
  Room 202
  Burlingame, CA 94010
  (415) 697-6835

Grocery Manufacturers of
America
  1010 Wisconsin Ave., NW,
  Suite 900
  Washington, DC 20007
  (202) 337-9400

International Bottled Water
Association
  113 N. Henry St.
  Alexandria, VA 22314-2973
  (703) 683-5213

International Dairy-Deli-Bakery
Association
  P.O. Box 5528
  313 Price Pl., Suite 202
  Madison, WI 53705-0528
  (608) 238-7908

International Federation of
Grocery Manufacturers
Association
  1010 Wisconsin Ave., NW,
  Suite 900
  Washington, DC 20007
  (202) 337-9400

International Ice Cream
Association
  888 16th St., NW, 2nd Floor
  Washington, DC 20006-4103
  (202) 296-4250

International Mass Retail
Association
  1901 Pennsylvania Ave., NW,
  10th Floor
  Washington, DC 20006
  (202) 861-0774

Italian Wine & Food Institute
  1 World Trade Ctr.,
  Suite 2253
  New York, NY 10048-0202
  (212) 432-2000

Meat Importers' Council of
America
  1901 N. Fort Myer Dr.
  Arlington, VA 22209
  (703) 522-1910

National Association of
Beverage Retailers
  5101 River Rd., Suite 108
  Bethesda, MD 20816
  (301) 656-1494

National Association of Chain
Drug Stores
  413 N. Lee St.
  P.O. Box 1217-D49
  Alexandria, VA 22313-1417
  (703) 549-3001

National Association of Fresh
Produce Processors
  727 W. Washington St.
  Alexandria, VA 22314
  (800) 344-3300

National Association for the
Specialty Food Trades
  8 W. 40th St.
  New York, NY 10018
  (212) 921-1690

National Candy Brokers
Association
  P.O. Box 486
  North Andover, MA 08145
  (508) 685-3893

National Coffee Association
  110 Wall St.
  New York, NY 10005
  (212) 344-5596

National Dairy Council
  10255 W. Higgins Rd.,
  Suite 900
  Rosemont, IL 60018-5616
  (847) 803-2000

National Fisheries Institute
  1525 Wilson Blvd., Suite 500
  Arlington, VA 22209
  (703) 524-8880

National Frozen Food
Association
  4755 Lingleston Rd.,
  Suite 300
  P.O. Box 6069
  Harrisburg, PA 17112
  (717) 657-8601

National Food Processors
Association
  1401 New York Ave., NW,
  Suite 400
  Washington, DC 20005
  (202) 639-5900

National Ice Cream and Yogurt
Retailers Association
  1429 King Ave., Suite 210
  Columbus, OH 43212
  (614) 486-1444

National Juice Products
Association
  111 E. Madison St.,
  Suite 2300
  P.O. Box 1531
  Tampa, FL 33607
  (813) 273-6572

National Poultry & Food
Distributors Association
  604 Green St., No. 3
  Gainesville, GA 30501
  (404) 535-9901

National Soft Drink Association
  1101 16th St., NW
  Washington, DC 20036
  (202) 463-6732

National Yogurt Association
  1764 Old Meadow Lane,
  Suite 350
  McLean, VA 22102
  (703) 821-0770

Organic Trade Association
  P.O. Box 1078
  Greenfield, MA 01302
  (413) 774-7511

Pet Food Institute
 1101 Connecticut Ave., NW,
 Suite 700
 Washington, DC 20036
 (202) 857-1120

Popcorn Institute
 401 N. Michigan Ave.
 Chicago, IL 60611-4267
 (312) 644-6610

Shellfish Institute of North
America
 1525 Wilson Blvd., Suite 500
 Arlington, VA 22209
 (703) 524-8883

Snack Food Association
 1711 King St.
 Alexandria, VA 22314
 (703) 836-4500

Soap and Detergent Association
 475 Park Ave.
 New York, NY 10016
 (212) 725-1262

Specialty Coffee Association of
America
 1 World Trade Ctr., No. 800
 Long Beach, CA 90831
 (310) 983-8090

Tea Association of the USA
 230 Park Ave.
 New York, NY 10169
 (212) 986-9415

Wheat Foods Council
 5500 S. Quebec, Suite 111
 Englewood, CO 80111
 (303) 694-5828

How You Can Contact Phil Lempert

I would love to hear from you and receive your comments and supermarket experiences. Here's how!

Each Wednesday you can join me and my special guests for a lively discussion of the hottest food news and trends. Wednesday nights at 8 P.M. EST on America On-Line, Lempert's Supermarket Checkout Chat is held in the Windy City II Chat Room of Chicago On-Line (keyword: COL Chat). This chat room is the perfect place to find the answers to your food shopping and marketing questions—and to share your opinions, gripes, helpful hints, and observations with other consumers who care about getting the most value for their money.

If you are not yet a member of Chicago On-Line or America On-Line, call (800) 922-0808, ext. 3729. You'll get 10 hours of free on-line use, and your first month's subscription fee is waived. After your first month, you will be billed $9.95 a month, which includes 5 free hours of use each month. (Additional hours are billed at $2.95 per hour.)

To contact Phil Lempert directly use E-mail: LempertP1@aol.com.

■ Win a **free** Trend Tracker T-shirt

Become part of our nationwide consumer panel and help identify new trends. If you think you are the first one to spot a new product in the supermarket, you can win a free Trend Tracker T-shirt. So we can verify whether you are a winner, send the empty package, including its UPC code, store location, and your evaluation of the product, to:

>Phil Lempert's Trend Tracker T-Shirt
>Tribune Company
>220 E. 42nd Street
>New York, NY 10017

If I can answer any of your questions or you would just like to say hi, write me!

>Phil Lempert
>*Chicago Tribune*
>435 N. Michigan Avenue
>Chicago, IL 60611

© 1995 Tribune Media Services

INDEX